THE COMPLETE BOOK OF
MEAT COOKERY
IN COLOR

RECIPES TESS MALLOS
PHOTOGRAPHY NORMAN NICHOLLS
ART DIRECTION DAVID WILLIAMSON
DESIGN DAVID WILLIAMSON

Paul Hamlyn
LONDON · NEW YORK · SYDNEY · TORONTO

PUBLISHED BY PAUL HAMLYN PTY LTD
176 SOUTH CREEK ROAD, DEE WHY WEST
NEW SOUTH WALES 2099
AUSTRALIA

© COPYRIGHT HAMLYN HOUSE PTY LTD 1970
FIRST PRINTED IN 1971
TYPESETTING BY COMPUTYPE
PRINTED BY DAI NIPPON PRINTING CO., LTD. TOKYO, JAPAN

ISBN 0 600 07051 4

CONTENTS

FOREWORD

There are many recipe books available today so what is different about this one?

First of all this is a cookery book about meat—beef, veal, lamb, and pork. No custards or cakes in these covers!

Americans have always been interested in meat. Meat has been a focal point of our meals since the earliest days. when the grazing of livestock was the major occupation of settlers. Most Americans instinctively consider meat as the basis of a good square meal. Today's younger generation learn kitchen skills and household marketing in the supermarket age. The casseroles, roasts and braises of a generation ago are not to be found on crowded supermarket shelves.

The old, traditional recipes result in meat dishes with real flavour. In this book you will find a selection of interesting meat dishes suited to family meals and to entertaining with ideas for garnishing and what to serve with each recipe. Not all expensive, hard to prepare dishes, not all economical dishes, but family meat dishes to suit a range of tastes and pockets.

'The Complete Book of Meat Cookery' is more than a mere book of recipes. It explains the basic factors and gives guidance in selecting, preparing, cooking and serving meat and goes on to help you recognise the cuts of meat your meat retailer sells. It outlines the nutritional value of meat. It deals with the storage of meat in the home and it even explains the correct method of table setting.

'The Complete Book of Meat Cookery' is illustrated with attractive color photographs and helpful guides and charts on the cuts of meat. It is a 'must' for any bride and competent housewife. There are indeed a good many recipe books available today. But this one is different—maybe because it is more than just a recipe book.

BALANCED DIET

WHAT IS A BALANCED DIET

Eating is an essential part of our lives and yet few of us are fully aware of the nutritional value of the foods we eat. Whether we over-eat or try to eat a sensible diet, we still may not be getting sufficient of **all** the substances needed.

Food is the means whereby growth and repair of body tissues is maintained and various body processes are regulated. The correct choice of food helps to ensure good health throughout a normal life span.

Good health means more than just resistance to disease; it increases mental and physical efficiency, improves appearance and well-being and contributes to the physical heritage of future generations.

In this country there is a vast choice of food available to us and it is very easy to obtain in quantity and quality, but life in an affluent society, with a high standard of living, requires us constantly to keep in mind the need for a **balanced** diet.

We need a plan to help us select food wisely. Food can be divided into five groups according to the main nutrient each supplies. By choosing food daily from each of these groups a simple plan for a good balanced diet and good health can be followed.

MEAT, POULTRY, FISH, EGGS AND CHEESE

At least one serving with each meal, assuming there are three meals per day.

MILK

Children—at least one glass with each meal.
Adults—desirable minimum $\frac{1}{2}$-$\frac{3}{4}$ pint daily.

BREAD AND CEREALS

Preferably brown or wholemeal, 1-2 servings.

FRUIT AND VEGETABLES

At least one serving with each meal, including one raw, preferably a citrus fruit or tomato.

FATS

Butter, $\frac{1}{2}$-1 oz daily.

Ideally, each meal should contain a selection from each group. There are additional items such as sugar, flavouring, tea, coffee, etc. which can add interest and variety to our meals but are not wholly essential.

The chart below shows a simple yet satisfactory selection for the three daily meals.

BREAKFAST	fruit or fruit juice (if desired) cereal and milk and/or egg, meat or cheese toast and butter (if desired) coffee, tea or milk
LUNCH	meat, fish, egg or cheese brown or wholemeal bread and butter fruit and/or vegetable (raw or cooked) coffee, tea or milk
DINNER	meat or fish vegetables (two or more) fruit coffee, tea or milk

MEAT IS A SOURCE OF PROTEIN

The word 'protein' is derived from the Greek word 'protos', meaning 'first'. Protein is the first, or most important, ingredient (nutrient) in our diet. Man, unlike plants, cannot manufacture protein. It must be a part of our daily diet to maintain normal health. As man is an omnivorous animal, meat is the most natural food to provide his complete protein requirements.

Apart from high quality protein, many important substances are available in meat. They include minerals like iron, which is important for a healthy blood supply, and phosphorus, copper, sodium and potassium. Meat also contains several vitamins essential to good health.

MEAT IN THE AMERICAN DIET

The United States produce more meat than any other country. Almost the entire amount is consumed by its citizens. Beef ranks as the most popular meat, then comes pork, veal and lamb. Variety meats have their place in the average diet and it would be well to serve variety meats at least once a week because of the high nutritive value. Sausage-making was an early means of preserving meat, but the variety and flavor of these is so vast (because of foreign influences) that they are both a wholesome and interesting addition to the family menu.

MEAT AS A SOURCE OF PROTEIN, B VITAMINS, IRON

KIND OF MEAT	COMPLETE PROTEIN	'B' VITAMINS			IRON
		THIAMINE (B1)	RIBOFLAVIN (B2)	NIACIN	
Beef	Excellent	Fair	Good	Excellent	Excellent
Lamb	Excellent	Fair	Good	Excellent	Excellent
Veal	Excellent	Fair	Good	Excellent	Excellent
Pork	Excellent	Excellent	Good	Excellent	Excellent
Variety Meats (liver, hearts, kidneys)	Excellent	Excellent	Excellent	Excellent	Excellent
Sausages (frankfurts bologna)	Excellent	Fair	Good	Good	Good

All meat also contains the minerals copper and phosphorus in significant quantities

(All ratings based on cooked values)

BUYING MEAT

CONSUMER PROTECTION

Government regulations require fresh meat transported across state lines (to be sold commercially) to carry a federal inspection stamp. This is simply a control to reassure the purchaser that the fresh meat is both wholesome and processed under strict sanitary conditions. The stamp is inked with a vegetable oil which is completely harmless. Meat that does not qualify for federal inspection is covered by similar state regulations.

MEAT GRADING

Meat grading is voluntary, and different packers and retailers may use brand names to denote the quality.

The top grade of meat is U.S.D.A. PRIME, not always available in supermarkets and speciality stores, as it usually is sold to restaurants and hotels.

Grades normally found in supermarkets are:—

    U.S.D.A. CHOICE or
    U.S.D.A. GOOD

There are also two lower grades:—

    U.S.D.A. STANDARD and
    U.S.D.A. COMMERCIAL

though these are not often found on sale in the retail market.

These grades usually denote overall quality and tenderness. However, when meat is cooked to its best advantage, even the less tender cuts can be most delicious.

CUTTING UP THE CARCASE

Livestock, whatever the type, are not all meat. During processing from live animal to the product the housewife buys, a big proportion of the original weight is lost in non edible by-products, such as hides, skins, bone, and internal organs.

This loss continues through to the retailer, where individual cuts of meat are prepared from quarters of beef or sides of lamb, veal and pork. For example, a retailer is able to sell about 78% of beef from a steer U.S. choice. Similar ratios of meat to live weight apply to other domestic meat producing animals such as sheep and pigs.

PERCENTAGE OF RETAIL

Cuts from steer—U.S. choice

	%
Broiling cuts	13.25
Roasts	10.90
Braising Meats — (Pot Roasts)	36.68
Cook-in-liquid cuts	12.95
Ground meat	4.30
	78.08

Most meat bought from U.S. meat retailers is in a fresh, chilled state. This means that it has been kept at low temperatures just above freezing point. At these temperatures the tenderness of the meat actually improves during storage, due to quite natural processes providing it is kept under hygienic conditions. The meat retailer offers meat for sale shortly after delivery by his wholesale suppliers. He may select some beef, however, and store it in a chilled condition for some time, to sell to customers prepared to pay a higher price for 'aged' beef which acquires greater tenderness and flavour during 'ageing'.

Occasionally deep frozen meat is available through the retailer and, if still frozen, it may be stored in domestic deep freeze units until required for cooking. If carefully thawed it is equal in quality to fresh chilled meat. Refreezing thawed meat should be avoided.

HOW TO CHOOSE YOUR MEAT

Meat from young stock such as lamb, veal and yearling beef, tends to be more tender than mutton or beef from animals of a more mature age.

The amount of work done by a muscle while the animal was alive affects its tenderness. For instance the muscles in the sirloin and loin regions of a steer do less work than those of the leg and, as a rule, sirloin is superior in tenderness.

However, meats which are less tender, from more mature animals or parts of the animal which do more work, can be made tasty and tender by adopting the proper cooking methods.

Several other factors influence the choice of meat cuts.

Large families usually buy large joints of meat for roasting or pot roasting. These cuts, like the tender cuts suitable for broiling, are available only from a small proportion of the carcass. They are therefore in demand and so tend to be more expensive.

Various cuts of meat are more suited to meals for breakfast, lunch or dinner according to the way family meals are organised. There are special cuts suitable for barbecuing, cold buffets, picnics and for special occasions.

It is always worth considering the time available for the preparation of a meal when buying meat. As a rule the cheaper cuts require longer cooking time, but the larger cuts such as a joint for roasting, also require a long time. Steaks, chops and some variety meats are tender and can be quickly prepared. The cheaper cuts, however, can be just as tender and nutritious when cooked correctly.

The chart (right) shows the 'demanded' and economic' cuts of meat.

When buying meat it is important to be able to recognise good quality. With practice, you will soon judge the quality of the cuts in the meat retailer's window or in the display cabinet of the supermarket. The following guide will help you select the most suitable cuts from those available, according to your meal plan, family likes and budget.

	DEMANDED CUTS	ECONOMIC CUTS
BEEF	Porterhouse, Tenderloin, T-Bone and Rib Steaks, Sirloin Tip Roast, Standing Rib Roast, Rolled Rib Roast	Round, Flank, Blade and Arm Steaks, Rump Roast, Blade, Arm and Chuck Pot Roasts, Brisket (fresh or corned), Plate, Short Ribs and Cross cut shank
VEAL	Round, Sirloin, Loin and Rib Chops and Steaks, Leg Loin, and Rib Roasts	Arm and Blade Steaks, Arm, Rolled Shoulder, Blade Roasts, Riblets, foreshank
LAMB	Leg Steak, Sirloin, Loin and Rib Chops, Leg, Sirloin, Loin Rib Roasts	Shoulder chops Shanks and Breast Shoulder Roasts
PORK	Loin and Rib Chops, Loin and Fresh Ham Roasts, Cured and Smoked Ham	Shoulder Steaks, Arm, Picnic Chops, Boston Butt Roasts, Spare ribs, Bacon, Salt Pork, Hocks

HOW TO JUDGE GOOD QUALITY MEAT

BEEF GRADES: PRIME
CHOICE
GOOD
STANDARD } Rarely sold on retail market
COMMERCIAL

How to determine good quality fresh meat:	BEEF	VEAL	LAMB	PORK
Muscle	Grain: fine to medium Colour: Bright red (sometimes marbled with fine fat deposits when well finished)	Grain: Fine Colour: Pinkish-grey	Grain: fine velvety texture Colour: Pinkish-red	Grain: fine, close texture Colour: Light pink
Fat	Firm and creamy white	Soft and creamy	Firm, pinkish white	Firm, almost white
Bones	Creamy colour, Plenty of red marrow	Pinkish colour Plenty of red marrow	Small Plenty of red marrow	Pinkish Plenty of red marrow

HOME STORAGE

STORING MEAT

Meat, like other natural foods, is subject to spoilage and loss if it is not handled properly throughout all stages of preparation, distribution and storage. Because of the need to ensure that high standards of animal health and hygiene are maintained, meat is examined by Government inspectors during production. Premises and trading practices are governed by regulations designed to ensure the public receives a completely wholesome product.

The same high standards should be applied to the storage of meat in the home if it is to retain its freshness and best possible condition until prepared for the family meal.

THE REFRIGERATOR

The time that frozen, chilled or fresh meat can be stored in a refrigerator varies with the efficiency of the refrigerator and the temperature at which it is set. Although designs vary there is usually a special chilled or fresh meat compartment located in the coldest part of the cool storage area of the refrigerator. The three main storage areas of a domestic refrigerator are:

1a. Deep Freeze Compartment. Temperature —32°C or 0°F (Average).
1b. Freezer compartment. Temperatures well below 0°C or 32°F (below freezing point).
2. Cold storage meat compartment. Temperatures about — 2°C or 28°F (close to freezing).
3. Cool storage compartment. Temperatures + 2°C or 36°F (just above freezing).

REFRIGERATOR GUIDE

Quick-frozen wrapped meats for long periods. Freeze tightly wrapped fresh meats for long storage in moisture proof material-seal edges. Do not store processed or canned meats unless specified on package. Do not refreeze thawed or partially thawed meats. Do not store cooked meats.	Freezer compartment
Store fresh or prepackaged meat for short period only with wrappers removed or loose. Thaw meats from freezer compartment, allowing approximately 8 hours per pound—cook shortly after thawing. Store cooked meat (covered) for short periods only.	Cool storage compartment
Store fresh meat (uncovered or loosely covered) for short periods. Store cooked meats in airtight containers after rapid chilling (not freezing). Store processed or cured ready-to-serve meats.	Cold storage meat compartment

STORING FRESH-CHILLED MEAT

Most meat sold by butchers and meat retailers is fresh-chilled, held at a low temperature, but above freezing point. Fresh-chilled meat, including beef, veal, lamb, and pork should be stored uncovered, or loosely covered, in the coldest part of the refrigerator compartment (not the freezer compartment) or in the compartment designed for meat storage found in modern refrigerators. The temperature should be as low as possible without actually freezing the meat and air circulation should be maintained. 'Wet' meat will spoil rapidly from the growth of yeast organisms which are ever present in the air and which thrive in moist conditions, even at temperatures just above freezing point.

STORING PRE-PACKED-FRESH-CHILLED MEAT

Pre-packed meat, purchased from a chilled self service cabinet, should have the wrapping loosened or removed before storing in the refrigerator at above-freezing temperatures. Domestic refrigerators perform best when free air circulation is possible within the cabinet. Overcrowding the refrigerator should always be avoided if best results are to be achieved.

FREEZING MEAT

As a rule, if intending to store meat for long periods, it is best to buy it already frozen and transfer it quickly to a freezer to avoid thawing. Such meat has the advantage of having been properly wrapped and commercially quick-frozen at very low temperatures —far lower than can be achieved in domestic appliances.

If fresh meat is to be stored in the home for long periods, its storage life can be increased by storing it in the freezer compartment of the refrigerator. Only meat which is fresh and in top condition should be frozen. Meat will be no better in quality when it is removed from the freezer than when it was stored.

In all cases where meat is to be frozen, it is advisable to trim off any excess fat and remove bones where possible. The main rules when freezing meat are:

a) Conserve freezing space.
b) Ensure close wrapping to prevent loss of moisture and drying of the meat.
c) Avoid projections and prevent tearing the wrapping.
d) Achieve complete freezing in the minimum time.

Before placing wrapped portions of meat in the freezer, they should be labelled with the name of the cut and the date of freezing. Tightly wrap joints, or sufficient smaller pieces for one meal, in a moisture-vapour-proof material such as clear plastic sheeting. Individual portions may be kept separate by placing pieces of plastic sheeting between them, keeping the package flat to ensure rapid freezing. Expel as much air from the package as possible by ensuring close wrapping before sealing. Freeze meat quickly and hold at 0°C or lower. Most modern domestic refrigerators will give this temperature in the frozen food chamber. If long term storage is planned. Meat must be held at—0°F or 32°C, i.e. in a deep freeze.

STORING FROZEN MEAT

Some stores offer pre-packed, frozen meat for sale to customers who buy in bulk for storage in deep-freeze cabinets. It is important that hard frozen meat should not be allowed to thaw unless it is being defrosted for cooking.

Frozen meat should be stored in the freezer compartment of the refrigerator. It should be tightly wrapped for storage, following the same method given above.

Meat purchased in bulk in association with a food freezer plan is usually cut into joint size portions, wrapped and professionally frozen before delivery. Manufacturers of home freezers usually provide helpful instruction booklets on the operation of the equipment with wrapping and storage techniques. It is advisable to follow the manufacturers advice to ensure the best storage results.

Some authorities make firm recommendations as to the maximum storage life of various types of meat. Such recommendations depend on numerous factors, including the freshness of the meat at the time of freezing, effectiveness of wrapping and the performance of the freezer under variable conditions.

While the storage life of fresh meat under effective, below-freezing conditions is more than adequate for most domestic needs, appliance manufacturers should be consulted if long-term storage is contemplated.

THAWING FROZEN MEAT

Meat may be safely thawed before cooking. Most people prefer to cook fresh or thawed meat, believing it to have better flavour, tenderness and juiciness. However, it may be cooked from the frozen state provided adequate cooking time is allowed.

To thaw meat, place the frozen package in the cool storage compartment of the refrigerator and slit open the top of the wrapping. Thawing in a refrigerator may take up to 8 hours per pound, depending on the thickness of the meat. In cool climates, the meat may be thawed at room temperature, but it should be cooked as soon as thawing is complete.

It is normal for some moisture to escape from meat during thawing. This moisture can be disposed of by removing the moisture-proof wrapping during the final stages of thawing. The surface of the meat will quickly dry off to a fresh appearance when exposed to the atmosphere.

Neither partially thawed nor fully thawed meat should be re-frozen.

STORING COOKED MEAT

Cold roast meat makes a delicious meal. It is worth going to a little trouble when storing cooked meat in order to retain its flavour and fresh texture. As cooked meat is held at above-freezing temperatures, its storage life is limited.

Loosely cover and cool cooked meat at room temperature or cool in the refrigerator before storage. A certain amount of moisture will have already been lost during cooking, but further losses may be prevented if the cold meat is covered or closely wrapped before placing in the coldest part of the cool storage compartment of the refrigerator. Do not store cooked meat in the freezer compartment.

For best results and to preserve the flavour, store the cold roast meat in relatively large pieces, to be sliced when ready to serve.

Meat dishes, cooked by moist heat, can be prepared in advance, stored in the freezer compartment, and reheated when required.

STORING CURED MEATS

Uncooked, sliced, smoked or cured meats should be wrapped in greaseproof paper or open clear plastic and stored in the cool storage compartment of the refrigerator until required for cooking.

STORING MINCED MEAT, SAUSAGE AND VARIETY MEATS

Meats in this group, when purchased in a fresh-chilled state, should be prepared for cooking without undue delay. Between purchase and cooking, minced meat, sausage, liver, brains, kidneys, etc. may be wrapped and stored in the freezer compartment of the refrigerator, but they are better purchased close to the time when they are to be cooked. **Only fresh, frozen or cooked meat should be stored. Never store partially cooked meat.**

BASIC COOKING

ROASTING

Roast meat is so popular among the families of this country that it has become established as a traditional part of our cuisine. First-class meat, simply cooked by this method, gives us the delicious natural flavor of the meat which is difficult to surpass.

True roasting is, or used to be, cooking meat on a revolving spit in front of an open fire, with a pan placed underneath to catch the **drippings** from the meat. Today meat is roasted in an oven or in an electric frypan in most kitchens, so it is really being baked, but basting with the drippings is often part of the cooking process so we miscall it roasting. However, true roasting can still be done today on a spit which either revolves inside the oven or is combined with the broiler unit in certain models of modern cookers. Follow the manufacturers instructions carefully, if you have a spit, for delicious natural roast meat. If you are roasting meat in the oven there are several methods to choose from. Firstly the prepared meat is placed in a hot oven for a short time to **sear** or **seal** the surface, then the temperature is reduced to moderate and the meat continues to cook for the required time. The meat is seared in order to seal in the natural juices and retain the natural flavor but we know that the loss of juice is in fact the same with or without searing. However this method does produce a crusty tasty outside surface on the roast joint and helps to speed the cooking time.

Another method, which is perhaps the ideal, is to roast the meat in a moderately slow oven for the time required, basting occasionally. The meat tends to shrink less and is tender, juicy, with a delicious natural flavor, if not over-cooked.

Cheaper and tougher joints of meat for roasting are tasty and tender if cooked at a constant low temperature for a little longer than the normal cooking time.

A guide to roasting times and temperatures is given (right) but these will not always give the most perfect results according to personal taste and the quality of the meat. The only way to get the nearest to perfect result each time you roast your meat is to use a meat thermometer. Place the thermometer in the thickest part of the meat avoiding contact with the bone. Set the thermometer to the desired degree of cooking, i.e. rare, medium, well done, and roast for the time required.

Meat for roasting should be at room temperature to give the best possible flavour, so remove it from the refrigerator 30 minutes before cooking. Wipe the meat or scrape with a knife if necessary, but do not wash it. Weigh the meat and calculate the cooking time required (see chart at right), or insert meat thermometer. Season the fat selvege with salt and pepper, rubbing it in well with the fingers. It is not advisable to rub salt into the flesh as this may cause loss of juices during roasting. Set the oven at the correct temperature, with the shelf placed towards the bottom of the oven (follow the manufacturer's instructions carefully). Put 2-3 tablespoons of fat or oil into a roasting pan if the meat is very lean and place in the oven until it is smoking. Place the meat, fat side up on a rack in the roasting pan. Baste well to seal in the meat juices and place in the oven to cook. Cook according to weight, basting every 20-30 minutes to keep the meat moist until done. When cooked, transfer the roast meat to a serving platter and stand in a warm place for 15-30 minutes before carving. This time allows the meat to **set** and is therefore much easier to carve.

To baste. Take the roasting pan out of the oven and place on a board on your working surface, and close the oven door. Spoon the hot fat over the meat several times, with a large basting spoon. Return the meat to the oven and continue cooking.

ROASTING TIMES FOR MEAT

	Oven Temperature	Total Cooking Time
BEEF	325-350°F	Rare: 20 minutes per lb and 20 minutes over Well done: 30 minutes per lb and 30 minutes over
LAMB	325-350°F	25 minutes per lb and 25 minutes over
PORK	325-350°F	30 minutes per lb and 30 minutes over Thick cuts 40 minutes per lb and 40 minutes over
VEAL	325-350°F	40 minutes per lb and 40 minutes over

MEAT THERMOMETER CHART

MEAT	FARENHEIT
Poultry	190°
Fresh Pork	185°
Lamb	180°
Cured Pork, Veal and Beef, well done	170°
Beef Medium	160°
Beef Rare	140°

POT ROASTING

This is one of the best and simplest methods of cooking a cheaper joint of meat. It is a slow method of cooking which makes tough meat moist, tender and juicy. It is important to have the right type of pot or casserole. It should be of thick iron, enamelled cast iron, aluminium or flameproof pottery, big enough to hold a joint comfortably and with a close fitting lid.

Firstly the meat is browned all over in the pot. Brown the meat in 1-2 tablespoons fat if there is insufficient fat for browning on the joint of meat. Add an onion stuck with 2-3 cloves, a bouquet garni and salt and pepper. No liquid is added unless stated in the particular recipe and then it is usually not more than $\frac{1}{8}$ pint of stock or wine. Cover with the lid and place over a very low heat or into a slow oven to pot roast, allowing approximately 30 minutes to the pound.

Pot roast meat is served like roast meat with gravy which is full of flavor. Strain off the fat and add a little stock to the meat juices. The accompanying vegetables should be cooked separately to give the best possible flavor.

BROILING

Broiling is a quick simple method of cooking which is ideal for best quality tender small cuts of meat (see chart at right). Broiled meat is juicy, tender and full of natural flavor when served. Broiled meat is good to serve for the busy housewife in a hurry. It is also good to serve to those on a diet, for broiled meat has little fat and is delicious on its own without the addition of rich thickened sauces. Broiling requires a certain amount of attention to give the best results. For perfect results, meat should be broiled over a charcoal broiler or over red hot coals.

PAN-BROILING

Today, most housewives broil under a gas or electric broiler. Heat the broiler first until it is red hot. While it is heating heat the rack in the broiler pan underneath. If raw meat is placed on a hot rack it will not stick to it during cooking. Brush the meat with oil or melted butter, and sprinkle with pepper. Do not salt the meat as this causes the juices to run out thus losing some of the natural flavor and food value. Place the prepared meat under the red hot broiler and cook until it changes color from red-pink to brown (1-2 minutes). This means the surface of the meat has seared and the juices are sealed in. Turn the meat over and sear or seal the other side, then continue to broil for the required cooking time or until cooked. Turn the meat with tongs of two spoons to avoid piercing the seal. The broiler pan should be put lower down, farther away from the heat source, rather than reducing the temperature of the broiler, to give best results. Times for broiling meat depend on the cut, the thickness and on personal taste. When a cooked steak is pressed with your fingers it feels like a sponge if rare, is firmer and less spongy when medium, and quite firm with no give when well done.

Broiled steaks should be served immediately to be at their most delicious, however broiled chops and kebabs can be kept hot for a short time in the broiler pan with the juices, and the heat turned low.

PAN-FRYING

CUTS Meat at room temperature	BROILING TIMES IN MINUTES	
1. Sirloin Steak, 1 inch thick	Rare:	6-7
	Medium rare:	8-10
	Well done:	14-16
2. Porterhouse Steak ($1\frac{1}{2}$-2 inches thick, serves 2-3)	Rare:	7-9
	Medium rare:	10-12
3. T-Bone Steak ($1\frac{1}{2}$-2 inches thick, serves 2)	Rare:	7-9
	Medium rare:	10-12
4. Rib Steak ($\frac{3}{4}$-1 inch thick, serves 1)	Rare:	5
	Medium rare:	6-7
	Well done	9-10
5. Tenderloin (fillet mignon) (1-$1\frac{1}{2}$ inches thick, serves 1)	Rare:	6
	Medium rare to well done:	7-10
Château-briand (3-4 inches thick, serves 2)	Rare to medium rare:	16-20
Pork Chops		20-25
Lamb Chops ($1\frac{1}{2}$ inches thick)		15-20
Sausages	Thick:	10-15
	Thin:	8-10
Kidneys		10
Bacon	Slice:	3-4
	Rolls:	5-6

FRYING

Frying is a quick method of cooking. There are two methods of frying, deep fat and shallow fat frying. Meat is seldom deep fried except in the case of meat croquettes and Scotch eggs. Steak, chops and veal escalopes are often shallow fried. Meat is often shallow fried in the first stage of making stews, in braising and pot roasting. When frying meat, choose a fat or oil which complements the natural flavor of the meat, i.e. butter for juicy tenderloin steak and delicate wiener schnitzel, a mixture of butter and oil is ideal for most meats and the oil prevents the butter from burning, olive oil gives an authentic flavor to Mediterranean meat dishes, vegetable oil is used for Oriental meat dishes, ghee (clarified butter) is ideal for curries, lard adds to the delicious natural flavor of pork and clarified fat adds to the natural flavor of beef.

Frying is not always done in a frying pan in meat cookery, but often in a saucepan or flameproof casserole. Whatever vessel is used, it should have a heavy base which will distribute the heat evenly and fry the meat perfectly without burning or sticking.

When shallow frying meat in a frying pan, the fat should cover the base of the pan, and in some recipes it should come half way up the food, so that the sides are completely cooked, e.g. crumbed rib chops. Turn the food once only and remember that the surface of the food which is fried first is the most attractive for serving uppermost. If meat is thick it is cooked on a moderate heat after first browning on a high heat. The brown sediment left in the pan after frying meat is the concentrated meat juices. The excess fat should be poured off and the frying pan reheated with a little water, stock or wine and this gravy poured over the meat so that none of the tasty and nutritious juices are lost.

STEWING

Stewing is cooking food slowly and gently in liquid. Meat may be stewed either on top of the stove or in the oven. During stewing the liquid should simmer gently with bubbles just breaking the surface. Meat for stewing is usually from less tender cuts with a slight marbling of fat or gristle, and requires long, slow cooking. During stewing the gristle is changed into gelatine, which means the meat becomes tender, and the fat gives flavor to the stew. The liquid must not be allowed to boil rapidly or the meat will become tough.

Meat stews can be either brown or white. In a brown stew the meat is browned in fat and some flour is often added and browned to give extra color and flavor. Vegetables may also be browned to add to the color and flavor. Stock is added to come just below the level of the meat. The pan or casserole is covered and the stew is cooked gently on top of the stove or in the oven until tender. A flameproof casserole is ideal for cooking stews, but the preliminary frying can be done in a frying pan or large saucepan and transferred to an ovenproof casserole. The stew is served from the casserole.

In a white stew (often called a fricassée) the meat is not browned, but often blanched first to whiten it and remove strong flavors. A white stew is cooked on top of the stove and is thickened after the meat is cooked.

BOILING

Boiling is cooking food covered with water at boiling point. In the case of boiling meat, the joint is plunged into boiling, salted water and brought back to the boil to seal the outside and seal in the meat juices. The heat is then lowered and the meat is cooked in gently simmering water until tender. Allow 20-25 minutes per pound and 20-25 minutes over.

Salted meats should be soaked to remove some salt before boiling, or placed into lukewarm not boiling water.

When boiling meat for stock, soup or beef tea, it should be covered with cold water and allowed to stand 10-15 minutes, before heating, to draw out the juices from the meat. The meat should be cut into small pieces, to expose as much surface area as possible in order to extract as much flavor as possible into the liquid.

SAUTÉING

Meat used for sautéing must be young, tender and of best quality, such as beef, pork and veal tenderloin and tournedos.

Sautéing is frying meat lightly in a small quantity of butter and/or oil to seal in the juices. A small quantity of stock or wine is added to come level with the meat and this is simmered a little to reduce the sauce and concentrate the flavor. The sauce may be thickened at this point if desired.

A sauté pan should be used, which is a 2½-3½-inch deep straight-sided, heavy frying pan with a lid. The wide base allows room for browning and reduction of the sauce. The lid is used to slow down reduction of the sauce and ensures complete cooking of the meat. A deep frying pan with a lid may be used in place of a sauté pan.

BRAISING

Braising is an ideal method for cooking cheaper, tougher cuts of meat. Braising is a combination of steaming and baking as the food is cooked in a heavy pot on top of a 1-inch bed of vegetables with liquid to come a quarter up the side of the meat. The braise may be cooked on top of the stove or in the oven. A whole joint may be braised or meat may be cut into 2-inch squares and braised, in the case of ragoûts.

The meat is browned in fat in the pot firstly, then put aside. A mixture of root vegetables, cut in chunky pieces, is sautéed gently in the fat, with the lid on, for 10-15 minutes. This mixture of vegetables is called a **mirepoix** and is not served with the joint of meat. The meat is placed on top of the vegetables with the liquid and herbs and allowed to simmer for 2-3 hours on top of the stove or in the oven. The meat is served with the gravy strained and poured over it.

A heavy flameproof cast iron casserole is ideal for braising meat.

STEAMING

Steaming is a long, slow moist method of cooking food surrounded by steam rising from boiling water. Meat is often steamed first before roasting if it is a very tough joint, as steaming will make it more tender. Large pieces of meat are steamed in a steamer placed over a pan of boiling water. Small cuts of tender meat may be cooked between two heatproof plates over a pan of boiling water. The meat is easily digested and none of the flavour or food value is lost which makes this an ideal way to cook meat for invalids.

CASSEROLE COOKING

Casserole cooking is similar to pot roasting, but the meat is cut up and cooked in liquid. Other ingredients, vegetables, flavorings and herbs, are added to the meat and it is usually cooked in the oven. A casserole is served from the dish it is cooked in. This method of cooking requires very little attention and is ideal for either tender or tough cuts of meats, although the latter take a longer time to cook.

UTENSILS

FOR GOOD MEAT COOKERY

A wise cook will invest in good quality essential equipment for successful meat cookery rather than waste money on poor quality equipment that has to be quickly replaced or innumerable gadgets that are more than likely not used. Here is a list of equipment used for meat cookery and the photograph shows how attractive but hard wearing it can be.

FOR PREPARING MEAT DISHES

chinoise or conical strainer	3
chopper or cleaver	1A
chopping board	21
double boiler	
filleting knife	15
food chopper	16
French cook's knife	1B
kitchen scissors	15
meat pounder	2C
palette knife (spatula)	1C
pastry brush	
pepper mill	9
salt mill	
sieve or electric blender	
skewers	18
steel or knife sharpener	6
whisk	2A

FOR MEASURING AND WEIGHING

kitchen scales
measuring cup
measuring jug
measuring spoons

FOR COOKING MEAT

baking dish, fireproof, oblong
boiler or very large saucepan
broil pan with rack

casserole, fireproof or ovenproof, pottery, earthenware or enamelled cast iron	12, 17
cook's fork	1D, 4A
cook's spoon	4C
deep frying pan or electric fryer	
Dutch oven	8
egg slice (fish slice)	4B
entree dishes, fireproof, oval or round	20
frying pan with heavy base and lid or electric frying pan	7
kettle	12
ladle	5
meat roasting thermometer	14
pan stands	22
pie dish	19
potato masher	2D
pressure cooker	13
roasting pan with rack	11
saucepan with lid	10
saucepans	
skillet	7
wooden spoons	2B

FOR SERVING MEAT

carving board with spikes
carving fork
carving knife

BEEF

ROAST BEEF   E
ROAST TENDERLOIN OF BEEF
STUFFED ROAST BEEF
MIXED BROIL
CARPET BAG STEAK   1
BACON-WRAPPED
T-BONE STEAK BROIL   A
STEAK DIANE
STEAK AND MUSHROOMS
TOURNEDOS
STEAK AND ONIONS
BEEF STROGANOFF
ORIENTAL BEEF AND BEANS   C
BEEF GOULASH
BEEF STEW
BEEF CURRY   D
CARBONNADE OF BEEF
CASSEROLE OF BEEF
LANCASHIRE HOT-POT   J
RAGOUT OF BEEF
STEAK AND KIDNEY PIE   G
BEEF OLIVES   F

ROULADEN
POT ROAST OF BEEF
BAKED, GLAZED CORNED
   BRISKET
NEW ENGLAND BOILED
   DINNER
BEEF COBBLER
GROUND BEEF PIE
BRAISED OXTAIL
HAMBURGERS   B
CHILI CON CARNE
BOLOGNAISE SAUCE
MEATBALLS IN TOMATO SAUCE
SWEDISH MEATBALLS
MEAT LOAF
FRUITY CURRIED MEAT
   FINGERS
UPSIDE-DOWN BEEF PIE
SCALLOPED POTATOES WITH
   MEAT LOAF
BEEF FRITTERS
BAKED BEEF HASH

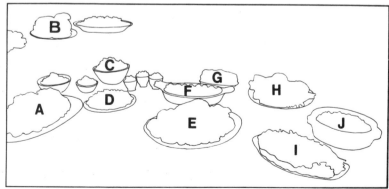

SOME AMERICAN RETAIL CUTS

HINDQUARTER
WHOLESALE CUTS

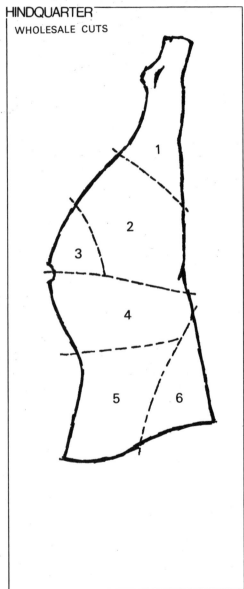

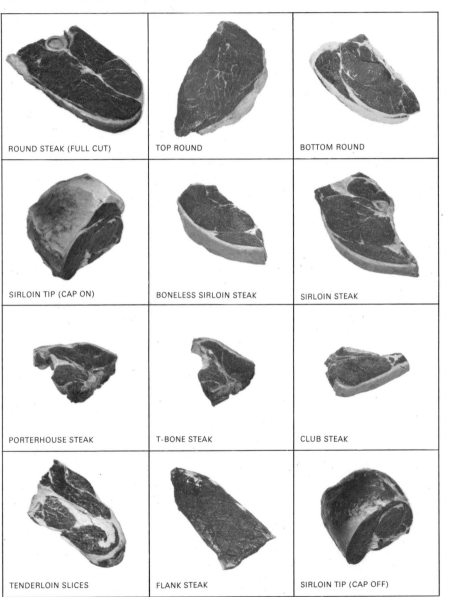

ROUND STEAK (FULL CUT)   TOP ROUND   BOTTOM ROUND

SIRLOIN TIP (CAP ON)   BONELESS SIRLOIN STEAK   SIRLOIN STEAK

PORTERHOUSE STEAK   T-BONE STEAK   CLUB STEAK

TENDERLOIN SLICES   FLANK STEAK   SIRLOIN TIP (CAP OFF)

BASIC CUT	RETAIL CUT	COOKING METHOD
1 HIND SHANK	Shank Cross cuts Heel of round	Cook in liquid (soup) Braise
2 ROUND	Round Steak (full cut) Top Round Bottom round	Braise Broil, pan-broil, Braise Braise
3 RUMP	Standing Rump Rolled Rump	Braise, Roast (high quality)
4 SIRLOIN	Sirloin Tip (cap on or off) Sirloin Steak Pin bone Sirloin Steak Boneless Sirloin Steak	Braise, Roast (high quality) Broil, pan-Broil Pan-fry
5 SHORT LOIN	Porterhouse Steak T-Bone Steak Club Steak	Broil, Pan-Broil Pan-fry
6 FLANK	Flank Steak (Rolled Flank and Flank Steak Fillets)	Braise (Tenderised it can be broiled)
7 TENDERLOIN (From 4 and 5)	Tenderloin Filet Mignon (Slices of Tenderloin)	Roast Broil, Pan-Broil Pan-fry

BASIC CUT	RETAIL CUT	COOKING METHOD
7 RIB	Standing Rib Roast Rolled Rib Roast Rib Steak Rib eye Steak	Roast Broil, Pan-broil Pan-fry, Barbecue
8 SQUARE-CUT CHUCK	Blade Pot Roast Arm Pot Roast Boneless Chuck English Cut Blade Steak Arm Steak	Braise Braise, barbecue, if pre-tenderised
9 SHORT PLATE	Plate Short Ribs	Braise, cook in liquid
10 BRISKET	Brisket (bone in or boneless) Corned Beef (Sometimes Rolled)	Braise, cook in liquid Cook in liquid
11 SHANK	Shank Knuckle Cross cut fore shank	Cook in liquid Braise

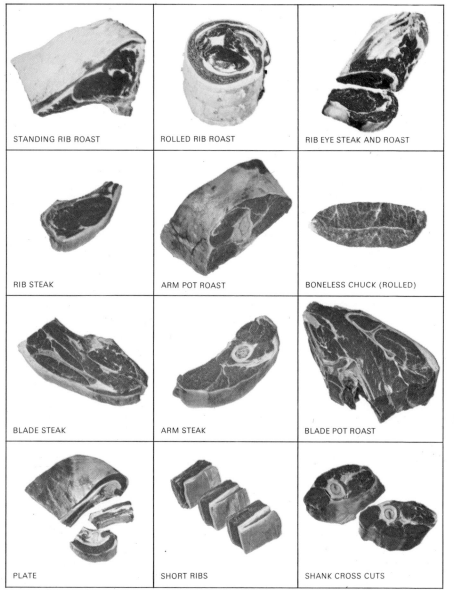

STANDING RIB ROAST

ROLLED RIB ROAST

RIB EYE STEAK AND ROAST

RIB STEAK

ARM POT ROAST

BONELESS CHUCK (ROLLED)

BLADE STEAK

ARM STEAK

BLADE POT ROAST

PLATE

SHORT RIBS

SHANK CROSS CUTS

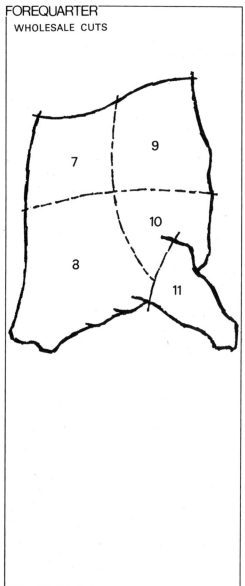

FOREQUARTER
WHOLESALE CUTS

7 9 10 8 11

ROAST BEEF

Serves 4-6
Cuts suitable for roasting are given on pages 18-19
1 x 3-4 lb roast of beef
salt and pepper
fat or oil

Wipe meat and weigh, calculate cooking time or insert a meat thermometer into center of flesh, (do not allow tip to touch bone or fat). Rub fat surface with salt and pepper. Place meat on a rack in a roasting pan, fat side up, unless the joint forms a natural rack, such as a standing rib roast. Place beef in a moderately slow oven and cook for about 30 minutes per pound or to the desired degree according to the meat thermometer reading (see page 11). Remove roast beef to a hot carving platter and leave to stand in warm place for 15-30 minutes before carving. This standing period makes it easier to carve the meat.
TIME 30-35 minutes per lb.
TEMPERATURE 325°F
GARNISH WITH Yorkshire Pudding (see page 76), roast vegetables, parsley or watercress.
SERVE WITH pan gravy (see page 72), Horseradish Sauce (see page 77) or mustard, roast potatoes and a green vegetable.
WHAT TO DO WITH LEFTOVERS, make into Beef Fritters, Baked Beef Hash (see page 29), or serve with salad or in sandwiches.

ROAST TENDERLOIN OF BEEF

Serves 6-8
1 x 4-5 lb beef tenderloin
melted butter or margarine
freshly ground black pepper
salt
1 lb small mushrooms
lemon juice

Trim fat from tenderloin, tuck thinner end under. Set oven at hot. Place meat on a rack in a roasting pan, brush with melted butter and sprinkle with pepper. Place tenderloin in hot oven and cook for 45-60 minutes, depending on taste. Insert meat thermometer in center to check stage of cooking if desired. When cooked, place beef on a heated carving platter. Fry mushrooms in a frying pan using the butter from roasting pan and add more if necessary.
Serve beef cut in inch-thick slices with fried mushrooms.
TIME 45 minutes-1 hour
TEMPERATURE 425°F
GARNISH WITH parsley or watercress.
SERVE WITH fried mushrooms, mustard or Béarnaise Sauce (see page 74), roast potatoes or jacket baked potatoes with sour cream, a green vegetable or a tossed salad.

ROAST STUFFED BEEF

Serves 6-8
1 x 4-5 lb sirloin tip (cap on) or rolled rump of beef
Herb and Bacon Stuffing (see page 75)
Pan Gravy (see page 72)

Cut a deep pocket into the beef. Wipe the beef with paper towels and fill the pocket with Herb and Bacon Stuffing. Close opening with small skewers or by sewing with string. Place beef on a rack in a roasting pan, fat side up, and cook in a moderately slow oven for 2½-3 hours. This time, 30 minutes to the pound gives you roast beef which is pink and juicy inside so cook for another 30 minutes for well done roast beef. Carve the stuffed beef and serve with gravy made pan drippings.
TIME 2½-3 hours
TEMPERATURE 325°F
GARNISH WITH parsley and roast potatoes.
SERVE WITH pan gravy, roast sweet potatoes or baked squash and onions and a green vegetable.

MIXED BROIL

Serves 4
Meats to choose from:
12 oz steak (for broiling)
4 small pork loin or rib chops
4 lamb chops
4 pork sausages
2 lamb's kidneys
4 bacon slices, rind removed
4 small tomatoes, halved

Choose at least three of the five meats listed. Wipe and trim steak and chops. Cut steak into four portions. Kidneys mush be washed, skinned, halved and the core removed. To prevent curling dur-broiling, skewer the halves of kidney on two skewers, 1-inch apart through each piece of kidney. Time the broiling of the meats by placing the meat which takes the longest to cook under the broiler first. Oil broiler rack and brush oil on meats. Preheat broiler to a high temperature and cook steak and chops quickly on each side for 1-2 minutes to seal the surface. Reduce heat for remainder of cooking time in order to cook the meat through. Turn meat, sausages and kidneys occasionally during broiling using tongs or two spoons to prevent piercing the meat, or the juices will escape. Cut bacon slices in half, roll up and place on a skewer. Place bacon rolls under broiler 6 minutes before end of cooking time. Broil tomatoes during last 3 minutes. Serve Mixed Broil immediately while piping hot.
GARNISH WITH parsley butter, sprigs of watercress or parsley.
SERVE WITH French-fried potatoes or hash brown potatoes and tossed salad.

CARPET BAG STEAKS

Serves 4-6
1-2 slices boneless sirloin steak,
(depending on surface area)
cut 2½-inches thick
½ pint oysters, drained
lemon juice
salt
freshly ground black pepper
2 tablespoons butter or margarine

Allow steak to stand at room temperature for 30 minutes. Make a slit through fat end of steak about 4-inches long and as deep as possible, using a sharp, pointed knife. Mix oysters with a squeeze of lemon juice, salt and pepper. Put oysters into the 'pocket' in the steak and secure slit with wooden toothpicks or a thin metal skewer 'weaved' through both sides of the slit. Preheat broiler to hot and brush rack with oil. Place steak on rack and spread surface of the meat with butter. Broil steak, 3-inches below heat, for 10-12 minutes on each side. For well done steak, reduce heat to moderate and broil for a further 5 minutes on each side. Spread more butter on steak during cooking and turn with tongs or two spoons. When cooked to desired taste, remove toothpicks or skewer and season the steak with salt and pepper. Serve Carpet Bag Steak sliced diagonally in slices 1-inch thick.
TIME 20-30 minutes.
GARNISH WITH watercress and grilled tomato.
SERVE WITH a green vegetable and French-fried potatoes, boiled new or baked jacket potatoes.

BACON-WRAPPED FILET MIGNON

Serves 4
4 slices tenderloin (filet mignon) steak,
1½-2-inches thick
4 slices rindless bacon
butter or margarine
salt
freshly ground black pepper

Wrap a bacon slice around each steak and secure with wooden cocktail sticks. Preheat grill to hot and brush rack with oil. Spread a little butter on each steak and place on grill rack 3-inches below heat. Grill for 3-4 minutes on each side for rare steak, 2 minutes longer each side for medium rare steak. Turn steak with tongs or two spoons to avoid piercing the meat and letting the juices escape. Season to taste with salt and pepper and serve immediately.
TIME 6-12 minutes.
GARNISH WITH parsley butter and sprigs of watercress or parsley.
SERVE WITH grilled or fried mushrooms, new, French-fried or shoestring and a green vegetable or a tossed salad.

T-BONE STEAK BROIL

Serves 4
4 T-bone steaks (or use porterhouse or rib)
melted butter or oil
8 large mushrooms
4 medium tomatoes
salt
freshly ground black pepper

Remove steak from refrigerator and allow to stand at room temperature for 30 minutes. Slit fat around edge in two or three places to prevent steak curling. Preheat broiler until hot, place steaks on oiled rack and brush lean surface of meat with melted butter or oil. Broil steaks for 2-3 minutes on either side to seal surface of meat, turning with tongs or two spoons. Reduce heat and cook for a further 4-6 minutes on either side. Place mushrooms on broiler rack during last 5 minutes of cooking time, brush with melted butter and replace rack under broiler. Add tomatoes, halved, 2 minutes after mushrooms and broil for a further 3 minutes. Turn mushrooms and tomatoes once during cooking time. Season steak, mushrooms and tomatoes with salt and pepper before serving.
TIME 14-20 minutes.
GARNISH WITH parsley butter, watercress and sprinkle with chopped chives.
SERVE WITH French-fried or jacket baked potatoes, a green vegetable or a tossed salad.

STEAK DIANE

Serves 4
4 slices tenderloin steak cut 1-inch thick
2 tablespoons butter
2 cloves garlic, crushed
salt
freshly ground black pepper
1 tablespoon tomato catsup
1 teaspoon worcestershire sauce
¼ cup water
1 teaspoon cornstarch
1 tablespoon finely chopped parsley

Slice steaks almost through the center and open out. Flatten steaks with the side of a meat pounder to ¼-inch thickness. Melt half butter in a heavy frying pan, add 1 crushed garlic clove and fry the steaks quickly—about 40 seconds each side for underdone steak and 1 minute each side for medium steak. Add remaining butter and garlic to the pan when completing the cooking of the steaks as most frying pans will probably hold only two steaks at a time. Season cooked steaks with salt and pepper and keep aside on a warm platter. Add sauces and water to frying pan and stir in the pan juices over a medium heat. Thicken with cornstarch mixed with a little cold water and bring to the boil. Add chopped parsley and pour sauce over the steaks.
TIME 2-4 minutes.
GARNISH WITH chopped parsley.
SERVE WITH new or sautéed potatoes, a green vegetable or a tossed salad.

STEAK AND MUSHROOMS

Serves 4
1½ lb broiling steak
½ lb large mushrooms
¼ cup butter or margarine
lemon juice
½ cup chopped green onions (optional)
salt
freshly ground black pepper

Cut steak into four pieces, unless purchased in four portions. Trim mushrooms and leave whole. Pan-fry steaks in 1 tablespoon butter over a high heat for 1 minute on each side to sear, continue cooking over a lower heat for a further 3-5 minutes on each side.
While steaks are cooking, melt remaining butter in another frying pan and place sufficient mushrooms in pan to make a single layer. Fry mushrooms quickly for 2 minutes on each side, turn, sprinkle with lemon juice and fry for a further 2 minutes. Lift out onto a warm dish and cook remaining mushrooms in the same method. Remove fried mushrooms and add green onions, if used, to the pan and cook until soft.
Sprinkle steaks with salt and pepper after cooking and serve with the fried mushrooms, spooning some green onions over each mushroom. Make a gravy from the steak pan juices if desired.
TIME 10-12 minutes.
GARNISH WITH chopped parsley if shallots are not used in the recipe.
SERVE WITH a green vegetable or tossed salad, new, mashed or sautéed potatoes.

TOURNEDOS

Serves 4
4 slices tenderloin (filet mignon) steak 1-1½ inches thick (cut from small end of tenderloin)
2 tablespoons butter or margarine
4 slices white bread
extra butter or margarine

Trim slices of steak into neat portions. Melt butter in a heavy frying pan, add steak and sear over a high heat for 1 minute on each side, reduce heat to medium and cook for a further · 4-5 minutes on each side—a little longer if steak is preferred medium done. Using a large cooky cutter, cut a circle out of each slice of bread, the same size as the tournedo. Fry circles of bread in extra butter until golden, (croûtes) drain well and keep warm. Place each tournedo on a croûte and serve as one of the following: Tournedos Rossini: Spread top of hot tournedos with liverwurst. Dilute pan juices with Madeira, add salt and pepper to taste, heat through and pour over tournedos.
Tournedos Chasseur: Sauté sliced mushrooms in pan in which steaks were cooked, adding more butter if necessary. Add 1 tablespoon chopped green onions, ¼ cup dry white wine, ¼ cup beef stock and salt and pepper to taste. Bring to the boil, stirring continuously. Simmer 1 minute and pour over tournedos.
TIME 8-10 minutes.
GARNISH WITH chopped parsley, sprigs of watercress or artichoke hearts.
SERVE WITH a green vegetable, thinly cut French-fried potatoes or game chips (potato crisps).
NOTE a tournedo is often served with a rasher of bacon around it.

STEAK AND ONIONS

Serves 4
1½ lb broiling steak
¼ cup butter or margarine
2 large onions, sliced
salt
freshly ground black pepper

Cut steak into four pieces, unless purchased in four portions. Melt butter in a heavy frying pan and fry onions until just soft but not browned. Lift onions out and put aside. Increase heat under frying pan and place steaks in pan, moving them occasionally so that they do not stick. Cook according to taste, searing steaks on each side for 1 minute, then reduce heat a little and continue to cook for 3-5 minutes on each side. Lift steaks out onto a warm platter. Return onions to pan over a medium heat and cook until brown, stirring continuously so that pan juices mix with onions. Sprinkle steak with salt and pepper and serve hot with onions spooned over.
TIME 20 minutes.
GARNISH WITH sprigs of parsley.
SERVE WITH a green vegetable and french fried, mashed or scalloped potatoes.

BEEF STROGANOFF

Serves 4
1½ lb tenderloin steak
¼ cup butter or margarine
1 large onion, thinly sliced
½ lb mushrooms, peeled and sliced
1½ teaspoons salt
freshly ground black pepper
pinch of nutmeg
1 cup sour cream

Trim fat from steak and cut into thin 'finger-shaped' strips. Melt 2 tablespoons butter in a heavy frying pan and sauté the onion until soft. Add mushrooms and cook 5 minutes. Place mixture in a bowl and keep warm. Melt remaining butter in pan and quickly brown beef strips on all sides. Do this stage in two lots, unless a very large frying pan is used. Take pan off heat, add onions, mushrooms, salt, pepper and nutmeg. Stir well to blend, replace pan over a medium heat and pour in sour cream. Heat gently until heated through. Do not allow to boil. Serve Beef Stroganoff immediately.
TIME 15 minutes.
GARNISH WITH chopped parsley.
SERVE WITH boiled rice or noodles and a tossed salad.
NOTE a cheaper, tasty version of this dish may be made using round steak, with the addition of ¾ cup water to the meat after browning. Cover tightly and simmer for 30 minutes, add previously sautéed onions and mushrooms, seasoning and nutmeg, cover and cook for a further 30 minutes or until meat is just tender. Thicken gravy with cornstarch blended with a little cold water, then stir in the sour cream.

ORIENTAL BEEF AND BEANS

Serves 4
1 lb top round steak
4 tablespoons oil
2 onions, quartered
½ lb green beans, cut into 1½-inch lengths
1 cup sliced celery
½ cup coarsely chopped sweet red or green peppers
1½ tablespoons corn starch
1½ tablespoons soy sauce
1 cup beef stock
¼ lb fresh mushrooms, sliced or 1 x 4 oz can mushrooms

Trim fat from steak and slice steak finely into thin strips about 3-inches long. (Partial freezing of the steak makes thin slicing easier). Heat oil in a frying pan and brown the steak strips quickly. Add onions, beans, celery and pepper and cook for 5 minutes, stirring constantly. Blend cornstarch smoothly with the soy sauce and stock and add to the pan with the mushrooms, stirring until the liquid is smooth. Reduce heat, cover pan with lid and simmer until beans are just tender (about 15 minutes). Cook a little longer if you prefer vegetables to be softer. Serve immediately.
TIME 20 minutes.
GARNISH WITH strips of sweet red and green pepper.
SERVE WITH boiled or fried rice.

BEEF GOULASH

Serves 4-6
1½ lb stewing beef
2 tablespoons oil or fat
2 onions, sliced
1¼ tablespoons paprika
1¼ tablespoons tomato paste
1¼ teaspoons salt
pepper to taste
½ teaspoon sugar
1 cup water

Trim beef and cut into small cubes. Heat oil or fat in a heavy saucepan and brown beef quickly on all sides (do this in two lots). Lift meat out and put aside. Reduce heat, add onion to pan and sauté until soft. Add paprika, tomato paste, salt and pepper, sugar and water. Bring to simmering point, return meat to saucepan and reduce heat. Cover tightly with lid and simmer gently for 1½-2 hours or until meat is tender and sauce has thickened.
TIME 1½-2 hours.
GARNISH WITH a sprinkle of paprika and chopped parsley.
SERVE WITH buttered noodles, boiled rice or sautéed potatoes and a green vegetable.

BEEF STEW

Serves 4-6
1½ lb stewing beef
2 tablespoons fat
2 onions, quartered
1 tablespoon all-purpose flour
1½ teaspoons salt
freshly ground black pepper
2 carrots, cut in chunks
½ cup sliced celery
1 small turnip, sliced
1½ cups hot water
cornstarch

Trim excess fat and gristle from beef, wipe meat and cut into neat pieces. Melt fat in a heavy saucepan over a high heat and brown the beef, adding just enough to cover base of pan. When browned on all sides lift out and brown remaining beef. Lift this out and keep aside. Add onions to pan and sauté over a lower heat until soft. Stir in flour and cook sufficiently to color flour golden brown. Return meat to pan with seasoning, carrots, celery and turnip. Add hot water, stir well to loosen any meat juices and flour which may have adhered to base of pan and bring to simmering point. Cover tightly and simmer over a gentle heat for 2 hours or until meat is tender. Thicken gravy with a little cornstarch blended to a smooth paste with a little cold water. Heat through before serving.
TIME 2 hours.
GARNISH WITH chopped parsley.
SERVE WITH a green vegetable and whole boiled, mashed or jacket baked potatoes.

BEEF CURRY

Serves 4-6
1½ lb stewing beef
2 tablespoons ghee (clarified butter) or vegetable oil
1 large onion, chopped
2-3 tablespoons curry powder
2 cloves garlic, crushed
1 x 1-inch piece fresh ginger root, grated or ½ teaspoon ground ginger
½ cup beef stock or water
½ cup coconut milk
1½ teaspoons salt

Remove excess fat from beef and cut into 1-inch cubes. Heat ghee or oil in a heavy saucepan and sauté onion until soft. Add curry powder, crushed garlic and ginger and fry gently, stirring mixture, for 5 minutes. Increase heat, add beef and cook for 3-4 minutes, stirring well during cooking. Add stock or water, coconut milk and salt, cover pan tightly and simmer gently, stirring occasionally, for 1¼ hours or until meat is tender and liquor has thickened. Serve hot.
TIME 1½ hours.
GARNISH WITH lemon and parsley sprigs and surround with a border of boiled rice sprinkled with paprika.
SERVE WITH boiled rice, sambals (see page 95), poppadums and chippatees (if available).
NOTE to make coconut milk: Place ¾ cup milk and ½ cup grated coconut in a small saucepan with a pinch of salt. Bring slowly to simmering point and strain through a fine sieve, pressing coconut firmly with a spoon to extract all liquid.

CARBONNADE OF BEEF

Serves 4
1½ lb stewing beef
2 tablespoons fat
2 large onions, sliced
1 clove garlic crushed
1 tablespoon all-purpose flour
1 cup beer
1 cup hot water
1 bay leaf and 2 sprigs parsley tied together
¼ teaspoon dried thyme
1½ teaspoons salt
freshly ground black pepper
pinch of nutmeg
2 teaspoons brown sugar

Wipe beef and trim off excess fat. Cut into large pieces. Heat fat in a heavy saucepan and brown beef pieces on all sides over a high heat. Remove from pan and put aside. Reduce heat to low, add sliced onion and sauté until soft, add garlic and cook a little longer. Stir in flour and cook sufficiently to color it golden brown. Pour in beer and hot water, stir constantly until thickened. Increase heat and simmer to reduce liquor in saucepan by half. Return beef to pan, adding herbs, salt and pepper, nutmeg and brown sugar. Cover tightly and simmer for 2 hours, stirring occasionally during cooking. Remove bunch of flavouring herbs before serving.
TIME 2 hours.
GARNISH WITH chopped parsley.
SERVE WITH buttered noodles, whole boiled or mashed potatoes and red or green cabbage.

CASSEROLE OF BEEF

Serves 4
1½ lb round steak
2 tablespoons fat
1 large onion, thickly sliced
2 tablespoons all-purpose flour
½ teaspoon sugar
2 carrots, cut into chunks
¼ cup sliced celery
1½ teaspoons salt
freshly ground black pepper
1 cup beef stock
1 teaspoon worcestershire sauce
Parsley Dumplings (see page 75)

Trim beef and cut into large pieces. Heat fat or oil in a flameproof casserole and brown the beef on all sides quickly. Add onion and cook over a medium heat for 5 minutes. Stir in flour and sugar and cook, stirring, until a golden color. Remove from heat and add carrots, celery, salt and pepper, stock and worcestershire sauce. Stir well to lift off any flour and meat juices from the base of the casserole, cover and place in a slow oven for 2 hours. Fifteen minutes before the end of cooking time, place parsley dumplings in rough balls on top of the casserole, making sure they do not touch the sides so that the heat can circulate. Replace lid and bake for a further 15 minutes. Serve immediately.
TIME 2 hours.
TEMPERATURE 300-325°F.
GARNISH WITH finely chopped parsley.
SERVE WITH a green vegetable and whole boiled or mashed potatoes.

LANCASHIRE HOT-POT

Serves 4
1½ lb blade, flank or chunk steak
2 teaspoons salt
freshly ground black pepper
2 tablespoons all-purpose flour
1½ lb potatoes
½ cup sliced celery
¼ lb mushrooms, trimmed and quartered
1 large onion, sliced
1 cup hot beef stock
melted butter or margarine

Trim beef and cut into 1-inch cubes. Mix salt and pepper with the flour and coat the meat in the seasoned flour. Slice enough potatoes to cover top of casserole to be used and cut the remainder into chunky pieces. Mix potatoes with the celery and mushrooms. Place a layer of sliced onion in the base of the casserole, cover with a layer of meat, then add a layer of the mixed vegetables. Repeat layers, finishing with a closely packed layer of rows of sliced potatoes, overlapping the slices for sliced potatoes, overlapping the slices for the best effect. Sprinkle any remaining flour over and pour over the hot beef stock. Brush sliced potatoes with melted butter or margarine, cover casserole with lid or use aluminium foil if no lid available. Place in a moderate oven and cook for 2 hours. Fifteen minutes before the end of cooking time remove lid to allow the layer of potatoes to become crisp and golden brown.
TIME 2 hours.
TEMPERATURE 325-350°F.
GARNISH WITH finely chopped parsley and tomato slices.
SERVE WITH a green vegetable.

RAGOÛT OF BEEF

Serves 4
1½ lb round steak cut 1-inch thick
2 tablespoons oil or butter
1 onion, chopped
2 cloves garlic, crushed
2 carrots, cut into thick chunks
2 stalks celery, sliced in 1-inch pieces
1 cup skinned, chopped tomatoes
1 tablespoon tomato paste
1 bay leaf
1 onion studded with 3 cloves
1 cup beef stock or water
¼ cup red wine
1½ teaspoons salt
freshly ground black pepper
½ lb zucchini (courgettes), thickly sliced

Trim steak and cut into 1-inch cubes. Heat oil or butter in a flameproof casserole over a high heat and brown beef well on all sides. Lift out and put aside. Reduce heat, add onion and garlic and cook for 10 minutes. Add carrots, celery, tomatoes, tomato paste, bay leaf, clove-studded onion, stock, wine and seasoning. Stir well, return beef to casserole, cover and cook in a moderately slow oven for 1½ hours.
Add zucchini, return to oven for a further 30 minutes or until meat is tender. Remove clove-studded onion and bay leaf. Serve at the table from the casserole.
TIME 2 hours.
TEMPERAT-RE 325-350°F.
GARNISH WITH chopped parsley.
SERVE WITH a green vegetable or boiled rice, noodles, whole boiled, mashed or sautéed potatoes.

STEAK AND KIDNEY PIE

Serves 4
1 lb stewing steak
2 lamb's kidneys
2 tablespoons all-purpose flour
1 teaspoon salt
freshly ground black pepper
2 tablespoons fat
½ cup water
2 tablespoons chopped parsley
12 oz Flaky Pastry (see page 76)
or 12 oz commercial puff pastry

Trim steak and cut into ½-inch cubes. Wash and skin kidneys, halve and remove cores. Cut kidney into small pieces. Coat meat and kidney with seasoned flour. Melt fat in a heavy saucepan over a moderate heat and brown the steak and kidney, stirring continuously. Add water, cover tightly and simmer gently for 1 hour. Stir in parsley, leave to cool.
Roll out pastry 1-inch larger than top of pie dish. Cut a strip ½-inch wide from edge, place on dampened rim of dish, brush with cold water. Spoon steak and kidney into dish. Place remaining pastry over, press edges to seal. Trim off excess pastry and decorate edge by flaking and fluting with back of a knife. Glaze pie with beaten egg and cut a hole in top. Bake in a hot oven for 20 minutes, reduce heat to moderately slow and bake a further 20 minutes. Serve hot.
TIME 40 minutes.
TEMPERATURE 400-450°F reducing to 325-350°F.
GARNISH WITH parsley sprigs.
SERVE WITH mashed potatoes and a green vegetable.

BEEF OLIVES

Serves 4-6
3 thin slices top round steak
Herb and Bacon Stuffing (see page 75)
2 tablespoons fat or oil
1 onion, finely chopped
1 tablespoon flour
1 cup beef stock or water
1 teaspoon salt
freshly ground black pepper
pinch grated nutmeg

Trim all fat from beef, cut slices in half giving six pieces approximately 5 x 6-inches in size. Place beef between two pieces of clear plastic or waxed paper and beat until thin with a rolling pin or a meat cleaver.
Spread stuffing on each slice of beef, roll up and tie neatly with strong thread or white string. Heat fat in a flame-proof casserole or heavy saucepan and brown beef rolls quickly on all sides. Lift beef out and put aside. Lower heat, add onions to pan and sauté until soft, add flour and cook for 1 minute. Add stock or water, salt, pepper and nutmeg. Bring to simmering point, return 'olives' to pan and reduce heat to low. Cover tightly and simmer for 1½-2 hours or until meat is tender. Lift meat onto a hot serving dish and remove thread or string. Adjust flavour and thickness of gravy. Thicken gravy if necessary with a little blended cornstarch or reduce over a high heat. Pour over Beef Olives and serve hot.
TIME 1½-2 hours.
GARNISH WITH chopped parsley, diced cooked vegetables.
SERVE WITH a green vegetable and mashed potatoes.

ROULADEN

Serves 4-6
3 slices top round steak, thinly cut
German mustard (optional)
2 tablespoons fat
1 onion, chopped
1 carrot, chopped
1 stalk celery, chopped
1 cup beef stock
salt
freshly ground black pepper
Stuffing:
6 oz pork sausage mince or ground veal or pork
1 small onion, grated
2 tablespoons chopped parsley
½ teaspoon salt
freshly ground black pepper

Trim fat from beef and flatten out between two pieces of clear plastic with a rolling pin or a meat cleaver. Cut each slice in half and spread with German mustard. To make Stuffing, mix all together.
Spread stuffing on each piece of beef. Roll up and tie neatly with white string or strong thread. Fry the roulades in fat or oil in a heavy saucepan to brown all sides. Remove roulades from pan and add onion, carrot and celery. Sauté over a reduced heat for 10 minutes. Add stock and season with salt and pepper. Return roulades to pan, cover and simmer gently for 1½-2 hours or until beef is tender. Place roulades on a hot serving dish, remove string or thread and serve.
TIME 1½-2 hours.
GARNISH WITH chopped parsley.
SERVE WITH cabbage or sauerkraut and boiled new or mashed potatoes.

POT ROAST OF BEEF

Serves 6
1 x 4 lb beef pot roast
1 tablespoon fat
1 large onion, chopped
2 large carrots, cut in chunks
2 stalks celery, sliced
1 cup beef stock
2 teaspoons salt
freshly ground black pepper

Trim excess fat from meat, leaving a thin layer on the pot roast. Heat fat in a flame-proof casserole, Dutch oven or heavy saucepan over a high heat and brown meat well on all sides. Lift meat out, reduce heat, add vegetables and sauté until onion is soft. Add stock and seasoning and return beef to the 'pot'. Reduce heat when simmering point is reached, cover tightly with lid and simmer very gently for 2 hours or until beef is tender. Lift Pot Roast on to a warm serving platter, cover and keep warm. Reduce liquid in pot over a high heat until the sauce is thick. Either serve the sauce with the vegetables, spooning a little over the beef, or strain the sauce through a pointed strainer or sieve and serve in a sauceboat.
TIME 2 hours.
GARNISH WITH sprigs of parsley and braised onion and carrots.
SERVE WITH whole boiled potatoes.
NOTE a bunch of flavoring herbs may be added if desired, such as a sprig each of fresh marjoram and thyme. 2 sprigs of parsley and a bay leaf. Lift out and discard after cooking.

BAKED, GLAZED CORNED BRISKET

Serves 6-8
4 lb corned brisket
1 tablespoon mixed spice
1 onion, quartered
1 stalk celery, sliced
1 carrot, sliced

Glaze:
cloves
$\frac{1}{4}$ cup brown sugar, firmly packed
1 tablespoon dry mustard
$\frac{1}{2}$ cup orange juice

Rinse corned beef in cold water and place in a kettle. Add mixed spice, onion, celery, carrot and sufficient cold water to cover the meat. Bring to simmering point, cover and simmer for 3 hours. Cool beef in the liquid. Lift out beef, strain liquid and use for making soup.
Place beef in a shallow roasting pan and score fat with a sharp knife. Stud with cloves. Mix together brown sugar and mustard and pat on to the top of the beef. Pour fruit juice into the roasting pan and bake the beef in a slow oven for 1 hour, basting frequently with the pan juices. It may be necessary to pat on more brown sugar after 30 minutes. At the end of the cooking time the brisket should be well glazed. Serve hot or cold.
TIME 4 hours.
TEMPERATURE 300-325°F.
GARNISH WITH sprigs of parsley.
SERVE WITH baked pineapple or peaches, a green vegetable and new potatoes when hot, with salad when cold.

NEW ENGLAND BOILED DINNER

Serves 6-8
4 lb corned brisket
1 onion, quartered
1 small turnip, sliced
1 bay leaf
6 peppercorns
3 large carrots, quartered
6-8 small onions
6-8 medium potatoes
6-8 medium potatoes
6-8 cabbage wedges

Rinse brisket in cold water. Place in kettle and cover with cold water. Add quartered onion, turnip, bay leaf and peppercorns. Bring to a slow boil, cover tightly and simmer for 2 hours. Lift out beef, strain liquid to remove flavorings. Return liquid to kettle with beef and add carrots nd onions. Simmer for 30 minutes. Add potatoes and cabbage wedges. Cook until meat and vegetables are tender. Serve some of the broth with the Boiled Dinner.
TIME 3 hours.
GARNISH WITH the vegetables cooked with brisket.
SERVE WITH Tangy Mustard or Horse-radish Sauce (see pages 74 and 77) if desired.

BEEF COBBLER

Serves 4
2 tablespoons butter or margarine
1 onion, chopped
1 lb ground beef
$\frac{1}{4}$ cup finely diced celery
1 cup chopped mushrooms
$\frac{1}{4}$ cup beef stock or water
1 teaspoon salt
$\frac{1}{4}$ teaspoon pepper
$\frac{1}{2}$ teaspoon dry mustard
$\frac{1}{4}$ cup diced sweet red or green pepper
2 tablespoons finely chopped parsley
1 quantity Biscuit Dough (see page 75)

Melt butter in a frying pan and sauté onion until soft. Stir in minced beef and celery, increase heat and cook, stirring occasionally, until juices evaporate and the meat begins to brown. Add mushrooms and cook for 2 minutes. Reduce heat, add stock, seasoning and mustard. Simmer covered for 15 minutes or until liquid evaporates, stir in pepper and parsley and leave to cool.
Roll Biscuit Dough out to a rectangle $\frac{1}{4}$-inch thick. Spread cooled meat mixture to within $\frac{1}{2}$ inch of the edge of the dough. Roll up dough, moisten edges with water and press to seal. Lift onto a greased baking tray, brush with milk and sprinkle with sesame seeds. Bake in a hot oven for 15 minutes, reduce heat to moderate and bake for a further 15 minutes. Serve Beef Cobbler hot.
TIME 45 minutes.
TEMPERATURE 400-450°F reducing to 350-375°F.
GARNISH WITH chopped parsley.
SERVE WITH Curried Carrot Sauce (see page 74) and a green vegetable.

GROUND BEEF PIE

Serves 4
1 onion, chopped
2 tablespoons fat
1 lb ground beef
$1\frac{1}{2}$ cups beef stock
1 teaspoon salt
pepper to taste
$\frac{1}{2}$ teaspoon mixed, dried herbs
2 tablespoons chopped parsley
pinch of nutmeg
1 tablespoon worcestershire sauce
3 tablespoons all-purpose flour
1 quantity Plain Pastry (see page 75)

Sauté onion in dripping in a heavy saucepan until soft. Increase heat and add ground beef. Cook until the meat begins to brown. Add stock and stir thoroughly. Add seasoning, herbs, nutmeg and sauce. Cover saucepan and simmer gently for 30 minutes. Thicken beef mixture with the flour blended to a smooth paste with a little cold water and cool.
Take $\frac{2}{3}$ pastry and roll out to fit a round greased 8-inch pie plate. Place the cooled meat into the pie plate, moisten pastry edge, roll out remainder of pastry and place on top of pie. Press pastry edges firmly to seal, trim with a knife and decorate edge by fluting with fingertips. Decorate top of pie. Glaze pastry with beaten egg and bake in a hot oven for 15 minutes. Reduce heat to moderate and bake a further 25-30 minutes.
TIME $1\frac{1}{4}$ hours.
TEMPERATURE 400-450°F reducing to 350-375°F.
GARNISH WITH sprigs of parsley.
SERVE WITH baked tomatoes, a green vegetable and mashed potatoes.

BRAISED OXTAIL

Serves 4
2 lb oxtails
2 tablespoons flour
$1\frac{1}{2}$ teaspoons salt
freshly ground black pepper
2 tablespoons fat
2 onions, sliced
1 clove garlic, chopped
1 cup diced carrots
$\frac{1}{2}$ cup diced celery
$\frac{1}{2}$ cup diced turnip
2 cups skinned, chopped tomatoes
1 bay leaf

Ask butcher to cut oxtail into 2-inch slices. Rinse in cold water and dry. Coat in seasoned flour and brown in hot dripping in a heavy pan (with lid). Lift out and reduce heat. Sauté onions and garlic until onion is soft. Add carrots, celery, turnips and tomatoes and cook for a further 5 minutes. Return oxtail to pan, add bay leaf, cover and simmer gently for $2\frac{1}{2}$-3 hours, adding a little water during cooking if necessary. Serve hot.
TIME $2\frac{1}{2}$-3 hours.
GARNISH WITH chopped parsley.
SERVE WITH creamed potatoes and root vegetables.

HAMBURGERS

Serves 4
1 lb ground beef
1 teaspoon salt
$\frac{1}{4}$ teaspoon pepper
1 small onion grated or finely chopped
oil for dripping for frying
4-8 hamburger buns
onion slices, tomato and lettuce for serving.

Mix ground beef lightly with seasoning and onion. Too much handling causes meat juices to run out more freely and escape in cooking. If thick hamburgers are desired, form into four large patties, shaping meat lightly and quickly. Divide mixture into eight flat patties if well cooked hamburgers are preferred. Fry patties in a little hot oil or fat in a heavy pan or on a griddle. Cook thick patties for 5-8 minutes, depending on taste; thin patties take about 4 minutes. To serve, place Hamburgers in toasted buns and serve hot.
TIME 4-8 minutes.
GARNISH WITH onion rings (raw or fried), slices of tomato and a lettuce leaf on top of meat.
SERVE WITH German mustard, tomato catsup or chutney.
VARIATIONS
Cheeseburgers: Place cooked patty on base of bun, add sliced cheddar cheese and place under a hot broiler until lightly browned.
Herbed Burgers: Mix 1 tablespoon chopped parsley, $\frac{1}{4}$ teaspoon each thyme and marjoram and 1 teaspoon lemon juice into basic meat mixture.

CHILLI CON CARNE

Serves 4-6
1 onion, chopped
2 cloves garlic, crushed
1 tablespoon oil
1 lb ground beef
1 x 10 oz can condensed tomato soup
1 teaspoon salt
1 tablespoon chili powder
$\frac{1}{2}$ cup water
1 green pepper, chopped
2 cups cooked red kidney beans
or 1 x 1 lb can kidney beans, drained

Sauté onion and garlic in hot oil in a heavy frying pan. Add minced beef, increase heat, and cook until beef browns, stirring constantly. Add soup, salt, chili powder and water. Cover and simmer for 10 minutes, stirring occasionally. Add pepper and beans, simmer for a further 20 minutes and serve hot.
TIME 1 hour.
GARNISH WITH chopped parsley.
SERVE WITH boiled rice and a tossed green salad.

BOLOGNAISE SAUCE

Serves 4-6
2 tablespoons oil or $\frac{1}{4}$ cup butter
1 onion, chopped
2 cloves garlic, crushed
1 lb ground beef
1 carrot, finely chopped
$\frac{1}{2}$ green pepper, diced (optional)
4 oz mushrooms, trimmed and sliced
1 x 1 lb can tomatoes, chopped
or $1\frac{1}{2}$ cups fresh skinned, chopped tomatoes
3 tablespoons tomato paste
$\frac{1}{2}$ cup dry white wine
1 teaspoon dried basil
1 tablespoon finely chopped parsley stalks
$1\frac{1}{2}$ teaspoons salt
freshly ground black pepper
1 teaspoon sugar

Heat oil in a frying pan and sauté onion until soft. Add garlic and cook for 1 minute. Increase heat, add ground beef and cook over a high heat, stirring continuously, until meat juices evaporate and meat begins to brown. Add carrot, pepper and mushrooms if used, tomatoes, tomato paste, wine, herbs, seasoning and sugar. Stir to blend well and if mixture looks rather dry add $\frac{1}{2}$ cup water. Cover pan tightly, reduce heat and simmer sauce for 1 hour. Stir occasionally during cooking to lift any meat sediment from initial browning.
TIME 1 hour.
GARNISH WITH a sprinkle of finely grated Parmesan cheese.
SERVE WITH boiled spaghetti or use in other pasta dishes such as Lasagne.

MEATBALLS IN TOMATO SAUCE

Serves 4
Meatballs:
1 lb ground beef
1 onion, grated
½ cup dry breadcrumbs
2 tablespoons finely chopped parsley
1 teaspoon salt
freshly ground black pepper
1 egg
oil for frying
Tomato Sauce:
2 tablespoons oil from fried meatballs
1 onion, chopped
2 cloves garlic, crushed
1 cup chopped, canned tomatoes
or 1 cup fresh skinned, chopped tomatoes
3 tablespoons tomato paste
1 tablespoon tomato catsup
1½ teaspoons salt
freshly ground black pepper
½ teaspoon sugar
¼ cup dry white wine
¼ cup water

Mix ingredients for Meatballs together. With moist hands shape mixture into balls the size of a large walnut. Heat ½-inch oil in a heavy frying pan and fry meatballs quickly, browning all over. Litt out and drain.
To make Tomato Sauce, drain off all but 2 tablespoons oil from frying pan used for meatballs, add onion and garlic and sauté over a low heat until onion is soft. Stir in remaining ingredients. Bring to boil and pour over meatballs in saucepan. Cover and simmer 1 hour. Serve hot.
TIME 1 hour.
GARNISH WITH chopped parsley.
SERVE WITH boiled spaghetti.

SWEDISH MEATBALLS

Serves 4
½ cup dry breadcrumbs
¼ cup light cream or evaporated milk
1 lb ground beef
1 egg
1 small onion, grated
1 clove garlic, crushed (optional)
⅛ teaspoon ground allspice
1 teaspoon salt
freshly ground black pepper
¼ cup oil or fat
½ cup beef stock
cornstarch
½ cup extra cream

Soak breadcrumbs in cream or evaporated milk and combine with ground beef, egg, onion, garlic, if used, allspice and seasoning. Shape with moistened hands, into balls 1½-inches in diameter. Heat oil or fat in a heavy frying pan and brown meatballs on all sides. Drain off excess fat. Pour in stock and simmer, covered, for 20 minutes. Remove meatballs to a hot serving dish and thicken the remaining liquid with a little cornstarch blended with cold water. Heat through until boiling, add extra cream and cook over a low heat, stirring, for 1 minute or until hot. Pour sauce over meatballs and serve immediately.
TIME 30 minutes.
GARNISH WITH chopped parsley.
SERVE WITH a green vegetable and buttered noodles, rice, or mashed potatoes.

MEAT LOAF

Serves 4-6
1½ lb ground beef
¾ cup dry breadcrumbs
1 onion, grated
½ cup grated carrot
2 tablespoons finely chopped green pepper (optional)
¼ cup tomato purée
¼ cup mijk
1 egg
2 tablespoons chopped parsley
½ teaspoon mixed herbs
1½ teaspoons salt
freshly ground black pepper

Place minced beef in a mixing bowl. In another bowl blend together the breadcrumbs, onion, carrot, pepper, if used, tomato purée and milk. Stir in the beaten egg and herbs and seasoning. Combine the mixture with the minced beef and blend ingredients lightly together until well mixed. Spoon into a greased loaf tin and bake in a moderate oven for 1 hour. Drain off liquid, unmould onto a warm serving platter and serve.
TIME 1 hour.
TEMPERATURE 350-375°F.
GARNISH WITH chopped parsley.
SERVE WITH a green vegetable and mashed potatoes.
VARIATIONS
Tomato-Cheese Loaf: Unmould Meat Loaf as above, lay slices of cheese and tomato on top, return to oven until cheese melts and browns lightly.
Potato Frosted Loaf: Frost with 2 cups mashed potatoes into which 1 oz butter and 1 egg have been mixed. Bake for 15 minutes in a hot oven (400-450°F).

FRUITY CURRIED MEAT FINGERS

Serves 4
1 lb ground beef
¾ cup cooked rice
2 teaspoons curry powder
1 small onion, finely chopped
1 egg
1 teaspoon salt
pepper
½ cup raisins
flour
1 tablespoon fat
fruit chutney

Combine minced beef, rice, curry powder, onion, egg, seasoning and raisins. Mix well and with floured hands, shape into fingers approximately 3½ x 1½-inches in size. Melt fat in a baking dish and place bars in dish, brushing tops with melted fat. Bake in a moderate oven for 30 minutes, turning occasionally during cooking. When cooked, lift from dish and drain on absorbent paper. Serve hot, topping each meat finger with a heaped teaspoonful of fruit chutney.
TIME 30 minutes.
TEMPERATURE 350-375°F.
GARNISH WITH lemon butterflies and sprigs of parsley.
SERVE WITH Curried Carrot Sauce (see page 74), boiled rice and a green vegetable or sliced banana with lemon juice.

UPSIDE-DOWN BEEF PIE

Serves 4-6
1 lb ground beef
2 tablespoons fat, butter or margarine
1 onion, chopped
½ cup chopped celery
½ cup chopped green pepper
1 x 10 oz can condensed tomato soup
1 tablespoon worcestershire sauce
½ cup water
½ teaspoon salt
2 tablespoons chopped parsley
Biscuit dough (see page 75)

Brown ground beef in hot fat in a sauce-pan over a high heat. Add onion, celery and pepper, reduce heat and cook until onion is soft. Stir in tomato soup, sauce, water and salt. Heat through and keep hot while preparing Scone Dough. Place meat mixture into a greased, 11 x 7-inch rectangular cake tin. Roll out biscuit dough to fit the tin and lift carefully onto the hot meat mixture. Bake in a hot oven for 20 minutes. Invert onto a large serving platter and cut into squares to serve.
TIME 20 minutes.
TEMPERATURE 400-450°F.
GARNISH WITH parsley sprigs and fried onion rings or strips of blanched green pepper.
SERVE WITH a green vegetable.

SCALLOPED POTATOES WITH MEAT LOAF

Serves 4
1 x 10 oz can cream of mushroom soup
¾ cup milk
1 teaspoon salt
freshly ground black pepper
1½ lb potatoes, thinly sliced
8 x ¼-inch slices Meat Loaf

Mix together the soup, milk, salt and pepper. Pour a little of the mixture into a baking dish. Top with a layer of sliced potato, then cover with four slices of Meat Loaf (see page 28) and another layer of potato. Add half of the remaining soup mixture. Arrange a layer of potatoes and remaining meat loaf on top and pour the last of the liquid over all. Bake in a moderate oven for 1 hour. Serve hot.
TIME 1 hour.
TEMPERATURE 350-375°F.
GARNISH WITH a sprinkle of chopped parsley.
SERVE WITH freshly cooked green vegetables.

BEEF FRITTERS

Serves 4
8 slices cold beef
lemon juice
pepper to taste
oil for frying

Fritter Batter:
1 cup (4 oz) all-purpose flour
1 teaspoon salt
1 tablespoon melted butter or oil
½ cup plus 1 tablespoon lukewarm water
1 egg white
1 tablespoon chopped parsley

Sprinkle beef slices with a little lemon juice and pepper. Allow to stand for 30 minutes.
To make Fritter Batter, sift flour and salt into a mixing bowl and make a well in the center. Pour in melted butter or oil and stir in flour gradually with the back of a wooden spoon. Add water, a little at a time, and beat to a smooth batter. Fold in stiffly beaten egg white and parsley.
Dip meat slices into batter immediately and deep fry in a frying pan or in a deep fryer in hot fat or vegetable oil. When the fritter is golden brown on one side, turn carefully and brown the other side. Lift onto absorbent paper to drain before serving.
TIME 3-4 minutes for frying.
GARNISH WITH parsley sprigs.
SERVE WITH a freshly cooked green vegetable, tomatoes and new or mashed potatoes.

BAKED BEEF HASH

Serves 4
3 tablespoons finely chopped onion
2 tablespoons butter
2 cups diced, roast beef
2 cups diced, boiled potato
¼ cup dry red wine
¼ cup cream
¼ cup beef gravy or beef stock
2 tablespoons chopped parsley
pinch each of dried thyme and marjoram
salt
paprika

Sauté onion in butter in a frying pan until soft. Add diced beef and potatoes and gently fry, stirring, for 2 minutes. Stir in wine, cream, gravy or stock, herbs and salt to taste. Place in an ovenproof baking dish and sprinkle with paprika. Bake in a moderate oven for 20 minutes. Serve piping hot.
TIME 20 minutes.
TEMPERATURE 350-375°F.
GARNISH WITH a sprinkle of chopped parsley.
SERVE WITH freshly cooked green vegetables.

ROAST PORK
ROAST SUCKING PIG
ROLLED PORK ROAST
PORK CHOPS WITH APPLE
  AND PRUNES
FRUITY BAKED SPARERIBS
PORK CHOPS WITH ORANGE
POLYNESIAN PORK SATÉ
BROILED OR PAN-FRIED
  PORK CHOPS
CHINESE SWEET AND SOUR
  PORK
CHINESE FRIED PORK BALLS
FRENCH CASSEROLED PORK
PORK CHOPS IN WINE
CURRY GLAZED PORK CHOPS
PORK PAPRIKA
BOSTON BAKED BEANS
BAKED GLAZED HAM
SPARERIBS WITH CREOLE
  SAUCE
BARBECUED BUTT STEAKS
HAM RING WITH PEACHES
CREAMED HAM
CURRIED SAUSAGES
SCOTCH EGGS
TOAD IN THE HOLE
SPICY BAKED SAUSAGES
PORK JAMBALAYA
CREAMED PORK AND ONIONS
SAUCY PORK
SWEET AND SOUR PORK

PORK

SOME AMERICAN RETAIL CUTS

WHOLESALE CUTS

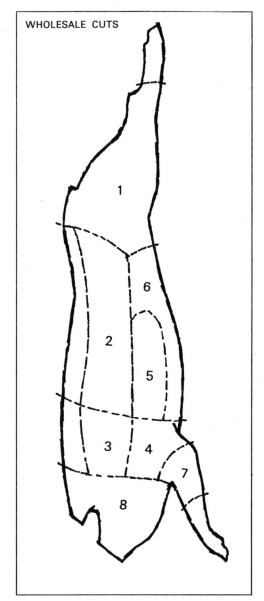

FRESH HAM (SKIN ON)

FRESH HAM-CENTER SLICE

CENTER LOIN ROAST

ROLLED LOIN ROAST

RIB CHOPS

SIRLOIN ROAST

FRESH BOSTON SHOULDER (BOSTON BUTT)

BLADE STEAK

FRESH PICNIC SHOULDER

ARM ROAST

ARM STEAK

SPARE RIBS

BASIC CUT	RETAIL CUT	COOKING METHOD
1 HAM (LEG)	Fresh ham (shank half)	Roasts
	Fresh ham (butt half)	
	Fresh ham (boneless)	
	Fresh ham (center slice)	Broil, Pan-broil, pan-fry, braise
2 LOIN	Sirloin Roast (bone in or boneless)	Roast
	Center Loin Roast (bone in or boneless and rolled)	
	Crown Roast	
	Blade Loin Roast	
	Tenderloin	Pan-fry, braise, broil, pan-fry, braise
	Sirloin Chops	
	Loin Chops	
	Rib Chops	
3 BOSTON BUTT	Fresh Boston Shoulder (or Boston Butt)	Roast
	Blade Steak (Shoulder chops)	Braise, pan-fry
4 PICNIC	Fresh Picnic Shoulder	Roast
	Rolled Fresh Picnic Shoulder	
	Arm Roast	
	Arm Steak (Shoulder chops)	Braise, pan-fry
5 SPARERIBS	Spareribs	Roast (Bake), Braise, cook in liquid
6 SIDE	Bacon	Broil, Pan-broil
	Salt Pork	Cook in liquid, Pan-broil
7 HOCK	Hocks	Braise, Cook in liquid
8 JOWL	Jowl bacon square	Cook in liquid, broil, pan-broil

ROAST PORK

Serves 4-12 depending on size
1 pork roast (see page 32)
oil and salt
Apple Sauce (see page 73)

If you like the skin of fresh pork cooked to a crisp, ask your meat retailer to give you the cut of your choice with the skin on. Have him score it in narrow strips.
For a crisp skin: Preheat oven to very hot. Rub skin of pork with oil and salt and place on a rack (skin side up), in a roasting pan. Cook pork in oven for 20-30 minutes to crispen skin. Reduce heat to moderately slow and cook for remaining time as calculated or insert a meat thermometer after first 45 minutes and cook as desired. (Meat thermometers should not be placed in an extremely hot oven). Do not baste as skin will toughen.
To cook a pork roast prepared in usual manner, season with salt and pepper and roast in a moderately slow oven, 325°F. Baste occasionally. Make gravy from pan juices (see page 72) and serve.
TIME 30-35 minutes per lb. for Loin cuts, 40-45 minutes per lb. for thick cuts such as fresh ham.
TEMPERATURE 450-475°F, reducing to 325-350°F. (for crisp-skin pork); 325°F for normally prepared pork.
GARNISH WITH baked apples, or spiced crab apples.
SERVE WITH pan gravy, Apple Sauce or cranberry sauce, roast vegetables and a green vegetable.

ROAST SUCKING PIG

Serves 10·12
1 x 18 lb sucking pig
oil
salt
1 small red apple

Stuffing:
6 lb pork sausage meat
2 apples
1 onion, finely chopped
1 teaspoon dried thyme
1 teaspoon dried rosemary
2 eggs
3 cups soft breadcrumbs

Wipe moisture from inside of sucking pig. Place stuffing in cavity and sew up securely with white string. Place a piece of wood or a meat skewer into the pig's mouth to keep it open. Rub surface with oil, then salt and rub again with oil. Place sucking pig in a large roasting pan and bake in a moderate oven for 4 hours, or until pig is cooked. The skin may be scored in a decorative pattern, if desired, before roasting. To serve, remove wood from pig's mouth and replace with a polished red apple. Serve hot or cold. To make stuffing, mix all ingredients together.
TIME 4 hours.
TEMPERATURE 325-350°F.
SERVE WITH Apple Sauce (see page 73) or cranberry sauce, jacket baked potatoes and salad.
NOTE a large roasting pan for roasting the pig may be made out of four layers of heavy foil.

ROLLED PORK ROAST

Serves 4-6
1 x 4 lb rolled pork loin or picnic shoulder
salt
freshly ground black pepper

Weigh joint and calculate cooking time. Wipe roll and rub surface with salt and pepper. Place roll on a rack in a roasting pan and cook in a moderate oven for 40 minutes per lb plus 40 minutes.
Lift roast pork onto a carving dish, keep warm. Make gravy from pan juices (see page 72) and flavor it with a pinch of herbs or a squeeze of lemon juice.
TIME 40 minutes per lb plus 40 minutes extra.
TEMPERATURE 325-350°F.
GARNISH WITH parsley sprigs.
SERVE WITH pan gravy, roast potatoes or sweet potatoes, roast root vegetables and a green vegetable.
WHAT TO DO WITH LEFTOVERS
see recipes page 31.

PORK CHOPS WITH APPLE AND PRUNES

Serves 4
4 pork rib chops ¾-inch thick, with pocket cut in fat side
½ green apple, peeled and thinly sliced
8 prunes, pitted and chopped
grated rind of ½ lemon
salt and pepper

Fill each pocket in chops with two slices of apple and some chopped prunes mixed with lemon rind. Close pocket with tooth picks and place chops in a roasting pan. Preheat oven to hot and cook chops for 10 minutes, turn, cook for a further 10 minutes. Reduce heat to moderarely slow and cook for a further 25-30 minutes or until meat is tender. Baste chops and turn occasionally during cooking. Season with salt and pepper after cooking.
To serve, remove toothpicks from chops and place on a serving dish. Keep chops warm and make gravy from the pan juices if desired.
TIME 45-50 minutes.
TEMPERATURE 400-450°F reducing to 325-350°F.
GARNISH WITH slices of apple fried in butter and some prunes stewed with lemon rind and a little sugar.
SERVE WITH new or mashed potatoes and a green vegetable.

FRUITY BAKED SPARE RIBS

Serves 4
2 lb pork spareribs
1 clove garlic, crushed
1 cup canned pineapple tidbits, undrained
2 tablespoons brown sugar
1 tablespoon vinegar
1 teaspoon dry mustard
1 teaspoon salt
freshly ground black pepper
½ cup orange juice
½ teaspoon allspice

Place spareribs in a baking dish in a hot oven on the shelf just above the center. Bake for 30-45 minutes to brown ribs (without burning) turning once during browning. Remove from oven and pour off as much fat as possible.
Mix together garlic, pineapple, brown sugar, vinegar, mustard, salt, pepper, orange juice and allspice. Pour mixture over spareribs and return to center shelf of oven. Reduce heat to moderate and cook, turning occasionally, for 45 minutes, or until meat is tender and glazed. Spoon off any fat before serving.
TIME 1¼-1½ hours.
TEMPERATURE 400-450°F reducing to 350°F.
GARNISH WITH chopped chives or green onions.
SERVE WITH boiled rice and a green vegetable or tossed, green salad.

PORK CHOPS WITH ORANGE

Serves 4
4 pork chops, loin, rib, blade or arm
grated rind of 1 orange
salt
freshly ground black pepper
¼ teaspoon curry powder
juice of 1 orange (about ½ cup)
2 teaspoons sugar
2 teaspoons cornstarch
1 tablespoon dry sherry

Rub grated orange rind into each side of chops. Place chops in a heated heavy frying pan greased with a little pork fat. Fry over a moderately high heat for 5 minutes on either side, reduce heat and cook for a further 10-15 minutes, turning once more during cooking. When cooked through, place on a hot serving platter and season with salt and freshly ground black pepper. Drain off fat from pan. Add curry powder to pan, cook for 1 minute, pour in orange juice and add sugar. Stir well and bring to the boil. Gradually stir in cornstarch blended to a smooth paste with sherry. Simmer until thick and bubbling, add salt and pepper to taste, pour over chops and serve hot.
TIME 20-30 minutes.
GARNISH WITH orange slices and sprigs of watercress or parsley.
SERVE WITH mashed potatoes and a green vegetable.

POLYNESIAN PORK SATÉ

Serves 4
1½ lb lean pork

Marinade:
1 onion, grated
1-2 cloves garlic, crushed
4 Brazil nuts, grated
¼ cup lemon juice
¼ cup soy sauce
1 tablespoon pepper
3 drops tabasco or other hot pepper sauce
1 teaspoon ground coriander
2 tablespoons brown sugar
2 tablespoons salad oil

Trim excess fat from pork, leaving some on and cut into 1-inch cubes. Combine marinade ingredients in a glass or pottery bowl and add pork pieces, mix well. Allow to marinate for 2 hours or more.
When ready to cook, thread pork on four metal or bamboo skewers and place under a hot broiler. Cook for 25 minutes or until cooked through (reduce heat after first 3 minutes on either side). Brush pork with marinade and turn often during cooking. Serve on a bed of hot rice. Heat any remaining marinade and serve over satés.
TIME 25 minutes.
GARNISH WITH parsley sprigs.
SERVE WITH boiled saffron rice or fried rice.
NOTE satés may also be cooked over a barbecue for outdoor eating.

BROILED OR PAN-FRIED PORK CHOPS

Serves 4
4 pork chops, loin, rib, blade or arm
oil
salt and pepper
apple slices, thickly cut
melted butter

Broiled: Preheat broiler to a high temperature until red hot and place chops on a greased rack. Broil chops for 5 minutes on either side, reduce heat to moderate and grill for a further 10-15 minutes, according to thickness and cut of chops. Place apple slices under broiler during last few minutes of cooking time, brush with melted butter, cook, turn, brush other side with butter and when tender serve as an accompaniment to the chops.
Fried: Heat a heavy frying pan, grease with a little pork fat and fry the chops over a moderate heat until browned on each side, continue cooking, reducing heat a little until cooked through (approximately 20-25 minutes). Drain off fat (lard) as it accumulates. Serve with apple and parsley sprigs.
TIME 20-25 minutes.
GARNISH WITH slices of grilled or fried apple and parsley sprigs.
SERVE WITH new, mashed or baked jacket potatoes, tomatoes and a green vegetable.

CHINESE SWEET AND SOUR PORK

Serves 4
2 cups cubed, cold roast pork
½ cup cornstarch
1 egg
2 tablespoons dry sherry
2 teaspoons soy sauce
oij for deep frying
Sweet and Sour Sauce
(see page 73)

Trim fat from pork before cutting into cubes and measuring. Mix together cornstarch, egg, sherry and soy sauce and add pork. Heat oil in an electric deep dryer or deep frying pan (not to fuming point) and deep fry pieces quickly, a few at a time. When golden lift pork out and drain well. Make Sweet and Sour Sauce according to directions on page 73 before cooking pork. Reheat sauce and pour over pork immediately it is cooked and serve with rice.
TIME 2-3 minutes to cook pork.
GARNISH WITH sweet red pepper slices.
SERVE WITH boiled rice and a freshly cooked green vegetable.

CHINESE FRIED PORK BALLS

Serves 4
1 lb finely ground pork
¼ teaspoon ground ginger
2 tablespoons cornstarch
1 teaspoon dry sherry
1 teaspoon salt
¼ teaspoon pepper
peanut oil for deep frying
Sweet and Sour Sauce (see page 73)

Mix together ground pork, ginger, cornstarch, sherry, salt and pepper until well blended. With moistened hands, shape into balls the size of a large walnut. Place oil in an electric deep fryer or a deep frying pan and heat oil well, but just enough so that when balls are dropped in they cook gently, though the oil bubbles. Fry pork balls until browned, lift out and drain. Just before serving fry again (this time oil can be a little hotter). Serve with Sweet and Sour Sauce.
TIME 8-10 minutes.
GARNISH WITH chopped chives, green onions or parsley.
SERVE WITH boiled or fried rice and bean sprout salad dressed in French dressing.
NOTE if using a thermostatically controlled deep fryer or frying pan, heat oil to 350°F.

FRENCH CASSEROLED PORK

Serves 4
1½ lb lean leg or shoulder pork
2 tablespoons butter or margarine
1 clove garlic
½ teaspoon dried sage
¼ pint hot water
1 teaspoon salt
freshly ground black pepper
2 teaspoons butter or margarine
2 teaspoons flour

Cut pork into 2-inch cubes. Heat butter or margarine in a heavy frying pan and brown pork on all sides over a moderately high heat. Do this in two lots if necessary. Add garlic and sage to pan during last part of cooking. Place pork in a casserole. Pour water into pan and stir well to lift pan juices. Add salt and pepper and pour over pork. Cover casserole and place in a moderately slow oven to cook for 1½ hours. Mix butter with flour to a smooth paste (beurre manié). Remove pork from oven and mix in butter/flour paste gradually until thickened (there will not be a lot of sauce). Heat through before serving.
TIME 1½ hours.
TEMPERATURE 325-350°F.
GARNISH WITH finely chopped parsley.
SERVE WITH new or sautéed potatoes and a crisp green vegetable.

PORK CHOPS IN WINE

Serves 4
4 pork shoulder chops
oregano
1 large onion, sliced
1 green pepper, chopped
1½ teaspoons salt
freshly ground black pepper
1 tablespoon tomato paste
1 cup skinned, chopped tomatoes
1 teaspoon sugar
½ cup red wine
cornstarch to thicken

Trim excess fat from chops and brown each side in a flameproof casserole or frying pan, greased with a piece of pork fat. Lift out and place in an ovenproof casserole if using a frying pan. Sprinkle with oregano to taste (about ½ teaspoon). Fry onion in pan until soft, add pepper and fry a little longer. Add salt and pepper, tomato paste, tomatoes, sugar and wine. Stir well to lift pan juices and either return chops to flameproof casserole or pour sauce mixture over chops in ovenproof casserole. Cook, covered, in a moderate oven for 1 hour or until tender. Thicken sauce, if desired, by blending 1-2 teaspoons cornstarch to a smooth paste with a little cold water and stirring it into the sauce in the casserole. Return to oven for 5-10 minutes to cook cornstarch, stirring now and then. Serve hot from casserole.
TIME 1 hour.
TEMPERATURE 350-375°F.
GARNISH WITH finely chopped parsley.
SERVE WITH boiled rice or pasta, or mashed potatoes and a crisp green vegetable.

CURRY GLAZED PORK CHOPS

Serves 4
4 thick pork loin or rib chops
(shoulder chops may be used)
1 onion, chopped
2 teaspoons curry powder
1 tablespoon flour
1 tablespoon brown sugar
1 teaspoon salt
½ teaspoon ground cinnamon
¾ cup beef stock
2 tablespoons tomato catsup
¼ cup puréed apricots and apples
(¼ cup dried apricots and 1 small apple
cooked and sieved)
1 tablespoon grated coconut

Trim excess fat from chops. Brown in a
large, heated frying pan, previously
greased with a little of the fat trimmings.
Do not cook chops through. Lift out,
drain on paper towels and place in a
single layer in a baking dish. Fry onion in a
little of the fat drippings in the frying pan.
Cook until soft, blend in curry powder and
cook slowly for 4 minutes. Stir in flour,
sugar, salt, cinnamon and stock. Continue stirring until sauce thickens. Blend
in tomato catsup, apricot and apple purée
and coconut. Spoon half mixture over
chops and place in a hot oven for 20
minutes. Turn chops and spoon over
remaining sauce. Bake for a further 20
minutes or until chops are tender and
richly glazed. Serve hot.
TIME 40 minutes.
TEMPERATURE 400-425°F.
GARNISH WITH slices of lemon and
parsley sprigs.
SERVE WITH baked sweet potatoes or
squash or boiled rice and sambals (see
page 95).

PORK PAPRIKA

Serves 4
1½ lb lean, boneless pork shoulder
lard or margarine
1 onion, chopped
2 tablespoons tomato paste
2 teaspoons paprika
1 teaspoon salt
½ teaspoon sugar
½ cup water

Cut pork into 1-inch cubes. Heat lard or
butter in a heavy saucepan and brown
pork pieces all over. Add onion and cook
over a moderate heat until browned a
little. Stir in tomato paste, paprika
salt, sugar and water. Cover and simmer
gently for 1¼ hours or until pork is tender.
Serve hot.
TIME 1¼ hours.
GARNISH WITH a sprinkle of paprika.
SERVE WITH mashed potatoes and
steamed cabbage.
VARIATION. reduce sauce after cooking,
until about ½ cup remains, stir in ¼ cup
sour cream and heat through gently
before serving.

BOSTON BAKED BEANS

Serves 4-6
1 lb dry navy beans
1 lb salt pork
2 cups liquid from beans
2 onions, chopped
3 tablespoons brown sugar
3 tablespoons molasses
2 teaspoons dry mustard
2 teaspoons salt
freshly ground black pepper
4 tablespoons tomato catsup
1 teaspoon worcestershire sauce

Soak navy beans in water overnight.
Drain. Place in saucepan, cover with cold
water and bring to the boil. Boil for 1
hour, drain, reserve liquid.
Pour boiling water over salt pork then
slash rind with a sharp knife in several
places. Cut pork into two pieces. Lay one
piece in a deep 2 quart casserole or bean
pot. Mix together onions, brown sugar,
molasses, mustard, salt and pepper. Stir in
2 cups bean liquid. Place beans on top of
pork, pour onion mixture over, stir and
place remaining pork on top, rind side
up. Cover and cook in a slow oven for 3½
hours or until beans are tender. Add
tomato and worcestershire sauces mixed
together and cook uncovered, for a further 30 minutes. If too dry add more bean
liquid. Serve Boston Baked Beans at
table from pot.
TIME 5 hours.
TEMPERATURE 300-325°F.
GARNISH WITH a sprig or parsley.
SERVE WITH pan-fried pork sausages.

BAKED, GLAZED HAM

Serves
1 Whole Ham (12-14 lb)—fully
cooked
1 x 1 lb can Pineapple tidbits, undrained
½ cup brown sugar
1 tablespoon dry mustard
½ cup canned pineapple juice
Whole cloves

Place ham, fat side up, in baking dish.
Place in moderately slow oven for 2
hours. Remove from oven and score fat
to depth of ¼-inch in diamond pattern.
Insert a whole clove in center of each
diamond. Mix pineapple tidbits, brown
sugar, mustard and pineapple juice. Pour
over ham in dish. Bake at 325°F for
further 1 hour or until meat thermometer reading is 130°. Spoon glaze in
pan over ham occasionally during cooking.
TIME 3 hours.
GARNISH WITH hot pineapple slices
studded with cloves.
SERVE WITH baked sweet potatoes and
squash and a green vegetable.

SPARERIBS WITH CREOLE SAUCE

Serves 4-6
2 lb Pork spareribs
2 tablespoons oil
1 large onion, chopped
1 clove garlic, crushed
1 green or sweet red pepper, cut in chunks
$\frac{1}{4}$ lb small mushrooms, trimmed
1 x 8 oz can tomato sauce
3 drops Tabasco sauce
$\frac{1}{4}$ cup water
salt
freshly ground black pepper
cornstarch

Place spareribs in a heated frying pan and fry until well browned on all sides. Lift out and drain. Drain off fat in pan, add oil and sauté onion until soft over low heat. Add garlic, cook a little, then pepper and mushrooms. Sauté for 5 minutes. Add sauces, and water and salt and pepper to taste. Return spareribs to pan, spoon over some sauce, cover and simmer gently for $\frac{3}{4}$-1 hour or until pork is cooked.
GARNISH WITH strips of pepper and parsley sprigs.
SERVE WITH boiled rice and a tossed salad.

BARBECUED BUTT STEAKS

Serves 6
6 slices smoked shoulder butt—1 inch thick
Marinade:
1 cup apple cider
$\frac{1}{4}$ cup melted butter or margarine
2 tablespoons dry mustard
2 tablespoons brown sugar
4 whole cloves

Lay butt slices in a glass or earthernware dish. Mix marinade ingredients together and pour over slices. Allow to stand at room temperature for 2 hours, turning occasionally. Broil under broiler or cook over glowing coals for 8-10 minutes each side, basting with marinade during cooking.
GARNISH WITH Apple Sauce and Watercress.
SERVE WITH baked jacket potatoes in foil and baked squash or tossed salad.

HAM RING WITH PEACHES

Serves 4-6
1$\frac{1}{2}$ lb ground leftover ham
$\frac{3}{4}$ cup dry breadcrumbs or fine cracker crumbs
1 egg
1 tablespoon grated onion
1 teaspoon prepared mustard
Pepper to taste
$\frac{1}{2}$ can syrup from canned Peach halves
butter
1 x 1 lb canned peach halves with remaining syrup

Mix ground ham with breadcrumbs or cracker crumbs, beaten egg, onion and mustard. Add pepper to taste, if necessary and blend in peach syrup. Place into a greased ring mould and bake in a moderate oven for 45 minutes. Unmould onto ovenproof platter.
Place peach halves in center of ring, dot with butter and brush remaining syrup over ham ring. Bake for further 15-20 minutes until ham is golden and peaches are heated through.
TIME 1 hour.
GARNISH WITH glazed onions.
SERVE WITH baked jacket potatoes, peas and hot rolls.

CREAMED HAM

Serves 6
2 cups diced, cooked ham
$\frac{1}{2}$ lb button mushrooms, trimmed
3 tablespoons butter or margarine
1 cup cooked green peas
$\frac{1}{2}$ teaspoon dry mustard
1 teaspoon lemon juice
2 cups Onion Sauce (see page 73)

Prepare diced ham and keep aside. In a frying pan sauté mushrooms in butter and lemon juice until tender. Add ham and mustard to pan and stir in peas and Onion Sauce. Heat through gently until piping hot, stirring occasionally. Adjust seasoning and serve.
TIME 25-30 minutes.
GARNISH WITH a ring of piped mashed potato and a sprinkle of paprika.
SERVE WITH a green vegetable.

CURRIED SAUSAGES

Serves 4
1½ lb pork sausages
2 tablespoons fat
1 large onion, chopped
1 clove garlic, chopped
1 tablespoon curry powder
1 tablespoon all-purpose flour
½ cup sliced celery
1 carrot, chopped
1 tomato, skinned and chopped
1 cup sliced green beans
1 cup beef stock
salt

Par-boil sausages by placing them in cold water in a saucepan and bringing them to simmering point. Remove from heat and leave standing in water for 10 minutes. Cut sausages into 1-inch slices. Heat fat in a deep pan and brown sausage slices on all sides. Lift out and keep aside. Sauté onion and garlic in pan for 10 minutes, stir in curry powder and flour and cook for a further 5 minutes. Add remaining vegetables, stock and salt to taste, stirring well. Bring to simmering point, cover and cook for 15 minutes. Add sausage slices and simmer, covered, for a further 15-20 minutes.
TIME 40 minutes.
GARNISH WITH parsley sprigs or young celery leaves.
SERVE WITH boiled rice and fruit chutney.

SCOTCH EGGS

Serves 4
6 hard-boiled eggs
1 tablespoon all-purpose flour
½ teaspoon salt
¼ teaspoon pepper
1 lb pork sausage mince
1 egg, beaten with 1 tablespoon water
dry breadcrumbs
oil or fat for deep frying

Coat hard-boiled eggs with seasoned flour. Divide mince into 6 portions. Shape each portion firmly and neatly around each egg. Brush with beaten egg and coat with breadcrumbs. Heat oil or fat to very hot, but not fuming, in an electric deep fryer or in a deep frying pan and deep fry Scotch Eggs. Fry gently as sausage meat has to cook through before the coating browns too much (takes about 5-7 minutes). When golden brown lift Scotch Eggs out and drain well. Slice in half lengthways before serving. Serve hot or cold.
TIME 5-7 minutes.
GARNISH WITH parsley sprigs.
SERVE WITH tomato catsup, mashed potatoes and a green vegetable when hot, with salad when cold.

TOAD IN THE HOLE

Serves 4
8 thick pork sausages
1 tablespoon fat
Yorkshire Pudding Batter (see page 76)

Place oven shelf just above center. Separate sausages and place in a baking dish with fat and heat in a hot oven until fat is very hot. Pour in Yorkshire Pudding Batter quickly and bake for 30-35 minutes or until batter is well risen and crisp and nicely browned.
TIME 30-35 minutes.
TEMPERATURE 400-450°F.
GARNISH WITH a sprig of parsley.
SERVE WITH baked tomatoes and a green vegetable.

SPICY BAKED SAUSAGES

Serves 4
1 · 1½ lb slim pork sausages
3 tablespoons tomato catsup
2 teaspoons worcestershire sauce
1 teaspoons dry mustard
2 teaspoons vinegar
1 tablespoon brown sugar

Split sausages almost through and place side by side in a greased baking dish. Mix together tomato catsup, worcestershire sauce, mustard mixed with vinegar and brown sugar. Spoon a little of this mixture into split in each sausage. Bake in a moderately hot oven for 20-25 minutes or until cooked (time depends on thickness of sausages as slim sausages vary in size).
TIME 20-25 minutes.
TEMPERATURE 375-400°F.
GARNISH WITH parsley sprigs.
SERVE WITH buttered rolls as Hot Dogs or with mashed potatoes and baked tomatoes.

PORK JAMBALAYA

Serves 4
1½-2 cups leftover roast pork
2 slices rindless bacon, chopped
2 onions, sliced
1 clove garlic, crushed
2 tablespoons butter or margarine
¼ cup dry white wine
1 x 1 lb can tomatoes
1 tablespoon catsup
½ teaspoon thyme
¼ teaspoon basil
¼ teaspoon paprika
2 drops tabasco sauce
2 teaspoons salt
freshly ground black pepper
½ teaspoon sugar
1 cup rice
1½ cups hot water

Trim most of fat from pork before cutting into cubes and measuring. Fry bacon in a frying pan (with lid) until almost crisp, add onion, garlic and butter. Cover pan with lid and sauté until onion is soft. Stir in wine, tomatoes, tomato paste, herbs, paprika, tabasco sauce, salt, pepper and sugar. Cook for 2 minutes, then stir in rice and hot water. Stir well to blend and cover tightly when mixture comes to the boil, reduce heat and simmer, stirring occasionally, for 25 minutes. Stir in pork and heat through. Serve immediately.
TIME 25-30 minutes.
GARNISH WITH chopped parsley.
SERVE WITH a freshly cooked green vegetable or a tossed salad.
NOTE: Cooked ham may be substituted for pork. Bacon can be left out and ham replaced in this stage of recipe.

CREAMED PORK AND ONIONS

Serves 4
1½-2 cups leftover roast pork, cut in strips
1 cup Onion Sauce (see page 73).
dry white wine
salt and pepper
paprika

Trim fat from pork before cutting in strips and measuring. Make Onion Sauce according to directions. Stir pork strips into the Onion Sauce and add enough white wine to give a creamy consistency. Heat gently without boiling. Add salt and pepper to taste. Serve in a heated dish and sprinkle with paprika.
TIME 15-20 minutes.
GARNISH WITH paprika.
SERVE WITH new or sautéed potatoes and a freshly cooked vegetable.

SAUCY PORK

Serves 4
1½-2 cups diced leftover roast pork
2 tablespoons butter or margarine
6 green onions, chopped
½ cup apricot juice
¼ cup tomato catsup
1 tablespoon cider or wine vinegar
2 teaspoons brown sugar
1 teaspoon worcestershire sauce
salt
freshly ground black pepper
¼ teaspoon allspice (optional)
2 teaspoons cornstarch

Trim fat from pork before dicing and measuring. Melt butter or margarine in a pan and fry green onions for 3 minutes. Stir in apricot juice, tomato catsup, vinegar, brown sugar and worcestershire sauce. Season to taste with salt and pepper and add allspice if used. Cover and simmer for 10 minutes. Thicken with cornstarch blended smoothly with a little cold water, stirring constantly. Stir in pork and heat gently, without boiling, until pork is heated through. Serve with hot, boiled rice.
TIME 15 minutes
GARNISH WITH chopped parsley.
SERVE WITH boiled rice and a freshly cooked crisp green vegetable.

SWEET AND SOUR PORK

Serves 4
2 cups cubed, cold roast pork
½ cup cornstarch
1 egg
2 tablespoons dry sherry
2 teaspoons soy sauce
oil for deep frying
Sweet and Sour Sauce (see page 73)

Trim fat from pork before cutting into cubes and measuring. Mix together cornstarch, egg, sherry and soy sauce and add pork. Heat oil in an electric deep fryer or deep frying pan (not to fuming point) and deep fry pieces quickly, a few at a time. When golden lift pork out and drain well. Make Sweet and Sour Sauce according to directions on page 73 before cooking pork. Reheat sauce and pour over pork immediately it is cooked and serve with rice.
TIME 2-3 minutes to cook pork.
GARNISH WITH sweet red pepper slices.
SERVE WITH boiled rice and a freshly cooked green vegetable.

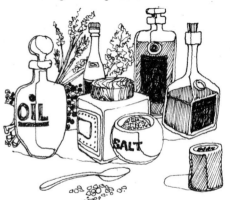

VEAL

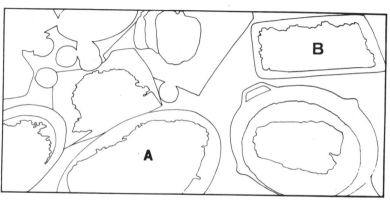

VEAL

SOME AMERICAN RETAIL CUTS

WHOLESALE CUTS

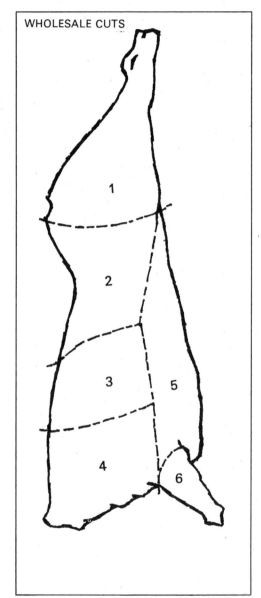

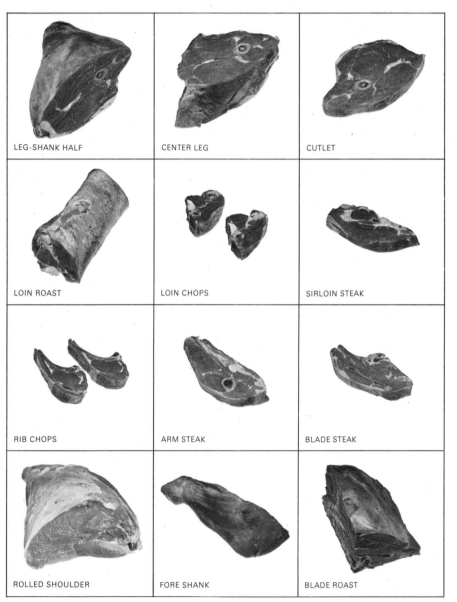

LEG-SHANK HALF   CENTER LEG   CUTLET

LOIN ROAST   LOIN CHOPS   SIRLOIN STEAK

RIB CHOPS   ARM STEAK   BLADE STEAK

ROLLED SHOULDER   FORE SHANK   BLADE ROAST

BASIC CUT	RETAIL CUT	COOKING METHOD
1 LEG	Leg Shank Half	Roast, Braise
	Center leg	
	Standing Rump	
	Cutlet (Round Steak)	Braise, Pan-fry
	(bone in or boneless)	
	Heel of Round	Braise, Cook in liquid
2 LOIN	Loin Roast	Roast, Braise
	Sirloin Roast	
	Loin Chop	Broil, Pan-fry
	Kidney Chop	Braise
	Sirloin Steak	
3 RIB	Rib Roast	Roast, Braise
	Rib Chop	Broil, Pan-fry,
	Frenched Rib Chop	Braise
4 SHOULDER	Arm Roast Rolled	Roast, Braise
	Shoulder Blade Roast	
	Arm Steak	Braise, pan-fry
	Blade Steak	
5 BREAST	Breast	Roast, Braise, Cook in liquid
	Riblets	Braise, cook in liquid
6 SHANK	Fore shank	Braise, cook in liquid

ROAST VEAL

Serves 4·6
Cuts suitable for roasting are given on page 42
1 x 3-4 lb joint of veal
freshly ground black pepper
4 tablespoons bacon fat
½ lb sliced bacon, rind removed
salt

Weigh joint of veal and calculate cooking time. Rub veal with pepper. Place on a rack in a roasting pan. Spread top with bacon fat. Place in a moderately slow oven and cook for calculated time. Alternatively, place meat thermometer in meatiest part with tip in center (not touching bone if the joint has bone) and cook until thermometer registers 170°F. Baste occasionally during entire cooking time. Turn veal over to brown other side during roasting. Fifteen minutes before serving, place bacon rolls (slices halved, rolled and placed on skewers) on rack next to veal and cook until lightly browned. Serve bacon rolls with veal, along with gravy made from pan juices (see page 72).
TIME 40 minutes per lb plus 40 minutes extra.
TEMPERATURE 325-350°F.
GARNISH WITH bacon rolls, parsley sprigs and lemon (optional).
SERVE WITH pan gravy, roast or new potatoes and a green vegetable.

STUFFED BREAST OF VEAL

Serves 4
1 breast of veal
Herb and Bacon Stuffing (see page 75)
salt
freshly ground black pepper
bacon fat, butter or margarine

For easier carving ask meat retailer to crack bones in veal and cut a long pocket in it. Stuff with Herb and Bacon Stuffing. Press wooden toothpicks through both sides of pocket and lace together to close with white string. Alternatively sew opening together with string or linen thread. Rub veal with salt and pepper. Place in a roasting pan greased with bacon fat or butter and spread more fat on top. Place in a moderately slow oven and cook for 1½ hours, basting occasionally. Make gravy from pan juices (see page 72) and serve hot.
TIME 1½ hours.
TEMPERATURE 325-350°F.
GARNISH WITH parsley sprigs and bacon rolls.
SERVE WITH pan gravy, roast or new potatoes and a green vegetable.

ROAST VEAL SHOULDER WITH FORCEMEAT

Serves 4·6
1 shoulder of veal, boned, unrolled
4 tablespoons bacon fat
freshly ground black pepper

Forcemeat:
2 oz ground beef suet
2 slices bacon or 2 oz ham, chopped
1¼ cups (about 4 oz) soft breadcrumbs
2 tablespoons chopped parsley
pinch of mixed herbs
rind of ½ lemon
salt and pepper
1 small egg

Open out veal shoulder and spread with forcemeat. Roll up, and tie into a neat roll with white string. Weigh joint to calculate cooking time or place a meat thermometer into center of roll. Rub meat with pepper and place on a rack in a roasting pan. Spread top with bacon fat. Cook in a moderately slow oven for calculated time or until meat thermometer registers 170°F. Turn meat during roasting and baste occasionally. Place roast veal on a warm carving tray and remove string. Make gravy from pan juices (see page 72).
To make Forcemeat, bind all ingredients with beaten egg.
TIME 40 minutes per lb plus 40 minutes extra.
TEMPERATURE 325-350°F.
GARNISH WITH forcemeat balls.
SERVE WITH pan gravy, roast potatoes and a green vegetable.

FOIL WRAPPED VEAL CHOPS
Veal Chops 'En Papillote'

Serves 4
4 x ½-inch thick veal chops
¼ cup butter
½ cup chopped green onions
1 clove garlic, crushed
½ lb mushrooms, trimmed and chopped
1 tablespoon lemon juice
½ cup dry white wine
1 large tomato, skinned and chopped
1 teaspoon tomato paste
¼ cup soft breadcrumbs
2 tablespoons chopped parsley
1 teaspoon salt
freshly ground black pepper
½ teaspoon sugar

Brown veal chops in 1 oz of butter in a heavy frying pan. Do not cook them completely. Remove from pan, reduce heat, add remaining butter and fry shallots and garlic for 3 minutes. Add mushrooms and lemon juice and cook for a few minutes longer. Stir in wine, tomato, tomato paste, breadcrumbs, parsley, salt, pepper and sugar. Cook until mixture resembles a soft paste (about 5-10 minutes). Cut some aluminium foil into rectangles. 10 x 12-inches. In center place an eighth of mushroom mixture, top with a veal chop, spread with another eighth of mixture. Fold foil over loosely, fold and press joins firmly to seal. Place on a baking sheet and cook in a moderately hot oven for 30 minutes. Serve chops immediately in the aluminium foil.
TIME 30 minutes.
TEMPERATURE 375-400°F.
GARNISH WITH parsley sprigs.
SERVE WITH new potatoes and salad.

WIENER SCHNITZEL

Serves 4
1 lb thinly cut veal cutlet, bone removed
1 clove garlic, crushed (optional)
1 tablespoon lemon juice
salt and pepper
flour
1 egg, beaten with 1 tablespoon water
dry breadcrumbs
oil or clarified butter (ghee) for frying

Flatten veal between two pieces of plastic wrap, using the side of a meat pounder or a rolling pin. Cut skin on edges to prevent curling during cooking. Lay veal on a plate. Mixed crushed clove of garlic (if used) with lemon juice and brush onto veal. Season with salt and pepper and allow to stand for 30 minutes. Dip each slice of veal into flour, then egg and finally breadcrumbs, pressing them firmly on to coat completely. Refrigerate for 1 hour. Shallow fry veal steaks in hot oil or clarified butter over a moderate heat for about 2 minutes on either side, or until golden brown. Lift veal onto absorbent paper to drain, then place on a hot serving platter.
TIME 3-4 minutes.
GARNISH WITH chopped hard-boiled egg white, sieved egg yolk, anchovy fillets rolled around capers, lemon slices and parsley sprigs.
 SERVE WITH new, mashed or sautéed potatoes, sauerkraut or a green vegetable or tossed salad.

GRILLED VEAL CHOPS

Serves 4
4 veal loin or rib chops
lemon juice or dried rosemary
butter
salt and pepper

Heat broiler on high until red hot. Place veal chops or cutlets on oiled broiler rack. Sprinkle veal with lemon juice or dried rosemary (rubbed first if it is in spikes). Top each chop with a small piece of butter. Place veal under hot broiler and cook for 2 minutes on either side. Reduce heat and cook for a further 3 minutes either side or until well done. Brush with melted butter occasionally during grilling as veal is deficient in fat. Serve immediately.
TIME 10 minutes.
GARNISH WITH grilled bacon rolls, lemon slices and parsley sprigs.
SERVE WITH new or mashed potatoes and a green vegetable.

VEAL WITH APPLE PURÉE
Veal au Boulanger

Serves 4
4 veal loin or rib chops
pepper
butter
salt
Parsley Butter (see page 77)

Apple Purée:
3 green apples
$\frac{1}{4}$ pint water
strip of lemon rind
2 teaspoons sugar

Preheat broiler at high until red hot. Sprinkle veal cutlets with pepper and spread each with a little butter. Place cutlets on oiled rack and broil for 5 minutes on either side or until well done. Place cutlets on a bed of previously cooked apple purée, sprinkle with salt and top each with Parsley Butter.
To make Apple Purée, peel and core apples and cut into slices. Place in a saucepan with water and lemon rind and cook until soft. Remove rind, mash apple well or press through a sieve. Stir in sugar and place on a heated serving dish. Keep warm while chops are grilling.
TIME 10 minutes.
GARNISH WITH chopped parsley.
SERVE WITH new or sautéed potatoes and a crisp green vegetable.

VEAL CORDON BLEU

Serves 4
8 medium sized veal steaks, cut from leg
4 thin slices of ham (about size of steaks
4 thin slices gruyère (Swiss) cheese
flour
salt
freshly ground black pepper
1 egg, beaten with 1 tablespoon water
dry breadcrumbs
oil for frying

Flatten veal steaks between two sheets of plastic wrap by beating with pounder or a rolling pin. Pair steaks together so that each piece is of a similar size. Place a slice each of ham and cheese between each pair of steaks, keeping ham and cheese $\frac{1}{4}$-inch from edge all round. Beat edges to seal. Coat veal with seasoned flour, brush with egg carefully, then coat with breadcrumbs, pressing them on firmly. Allow to stand 10 minutes, then shallow fry in hot oil over a moderate heat until a light golden brown, turn carefully and brown other side. It will take about 5 minutes to completely cook the veal. Drain on absorbent paper and serve piping hot.
TIME 5 minutes.
GARNISH WITH lemon wedges and chopped parsley.
SERVE WITH new, duchesse or mashed potatoes, a green vegetable or tossed salad.
NOTE if cheese leaks out of the steak and causes spitting, place a slice of potato in the pan to absorb moisture.

VEAL SCALLOPINE

Serves 4
1 lb veal steak, thinly cut
2 tablespoons flour
2 tablespoons olive oil or a mixture of
butter and oil
1 small onion, finely sliced
1 clove garlic, chopped
4 oz mushrooms, sliced
¼ cup sliced green pepper
salt
freshly ground black pepper
1 tablespoon lemon juice
¾ cup beef stock or water

Flatten veal steak with a meat pounder or
a rolling pin and cut into approximately
3-inch squares. Coat veal with flour. Heat
oil and butter in a frying pan and brown
veal slices quickly on either side. Do this
in two lots if pan is not very large. Add
sliced onion and garlic and cook a further
5 minutes. Stir in mushrooms and pepper,
cook a few minutes longer. Add salt,
pepper, lemon juice and stock or water.
Bring to simmering point, cover tightly
and simmer gently for 30 minutes or until
veal is tender. Stir Veal Scallopine occasionally. Serve hot.
TIME 30 minutes.
GARNISH WITH lemon wedges and
parsley sprigs.
SERVE WITH boiled rice and tossed
salad.

VEAL PARMIGIANA

Serves 4
1 lb veal steak, thinly cut
salt
freshly ground black pepper
1 egg beaten with 1 tablespoon water
½ cup dry breadcrumbs
2 tablespoons grated parmesan cheese
oil for shallow frying
Tomato Sauce (see page 28)
1½ teaspoons salt

Flatten veal steaks between two sheets of
plastic wrap, using a rolling pin or side
of a meat pounder. Season with salt
and pepper. Dip into beaten egg, then
coat with breadcrumbs mixed with parmesan cheese. Shallow fry veal steaks in
hot oil over a medium heat until evenly
browned on either side. No need to cook
right through. Drain fried veal on absorbent paper, and place in a single layer
in a reactangular, shallow, ovenproof dish.
Top with Tomato Sauce and slices of
mozzarella cheese cut in strips. Place in a
moderate oven and cook for 15 minutes or
until cheese melts and browns.
TIME 35 minutes.
TEMPERATURE 350-375°F.
GARNISH WITH chopped parsley.
SERVE WITH boiled rice, noodles or new
potatoes and a crisp green vegetable or
tossed salad.

BREADED VEAL CHOPS

Serves 4
4 Frenched veal rib chops
lemon juice
salt
freshly ground black pepper
flour
1 egg, beaten
dry breadcrumbs
oil for frying

Flatten veal chops with a meat pounder.
Sprinkle with lemon juice, salt and pepper
and leave for 20 minutes. Coat with flour,
then dip into beaten egg and finally
breadcrumbs, pressing them on to coat
well. Shallow fry coated veal chops in
hot oil in a heavy frying pan over a
moderate heat, turn when browned on
bottom and cook until other side browns,
about 8 minutes in all. Too high a heat
will burn coating. Drain on absorbent
paper before serving. Place paper frills on
bone ends.
TIME 8 minutes.
GARNISH WITH lemon wedges and
parsley sprigs.
SERVE WITH new or mashed potatoes,
a green vegetable or a tossed salad.

VEAL CHOPS PAPRIKA

Serves 4
4 veal loin or rib chops
2 tablespoons butter or margarine
2 teaspoons paprika
1 small onion, finely chopped
1 teaspoon tomato paste
¼ cup water
salt
freshly ground black pepper
1 teaspoon cornstarch
2 tablespoons cream

Melt butter in a heavy frying pan.
Sprinkle veal chops with paprika and
fry over a moderate heat until browned
and cooked through (about 10 minutes).
Lift out and keep warm. Lower heat and
fry onion in pan until soft, add tomato
paste, water and salt and pepper to
taste. Cook for 5 minutes over gentle
heat then thicken with cornstarch blended
to a smooth paste with a little cold water.
Bring to the boil, cook 30 seconds and
stir in cream. Replace chops in pan to
reheat, without allowing sauce to boil.
Serve immediately.
TIME 15 minutes.
GARNISH WITH finely chopped parsley.
SERVE WITH boiled rice, noodles, new
or sautéed potatoes and a green vegetable.

CASSEROLE OF VEAL

Serves 4
4 veal chops (arm or blade)
2 tablespoons all-purpose flour
1 teaspoon salt
freshly ground black pepper
2 tablespoons oil or butter
1 large onion, sliced
1 carrot
1 green pepper
$\frac{1}{4}$ cup white wine
$\frac{1}{2}$ cup beef stock
$\frac{1}{2}$ cup skinned, chopped tomatoes
2 tablespoons tomato catsup

Coat veal chops with seasoned flour and brown in half the butter in a flameproof casserole or a heavy frying pan. Keep aside (in the case of using the frying pan into an ovenproof casserole). Sauté onion, carrot and pepper with remaining butter over a low heat until onion is soft. Stir in remaining flour and cook until colored slightly golden. Add wine, stock, tomatoes and tomato catsup. Bring to the boil, stirring constantly, and return chops if using a flameproof casserole, or pour over chops in ovenproof casserole. Place casserole in a moderately slow oven and cook for 1 hour or until tender. Serve veal from casserole.
TIME 1 hour.
TEMPERATURE 325-350°F.
GARNISH WITH chopped parsley.
SERVE WITH mashed or new potatoes, boiled root vegetables or a green vegetable.

VEAL FRICASSEE

Serves 4
1$\frac{1}{2}$ lb stewing veal
$\frac{1}{3}$ cup butter or margarine
1 onion, quartered
1 carrot, cut in chunks
$\frac{1}{4}$ teaspoon thyme
1 clove
2 sprigs parsley
1 bay leaf
1$\frac{1}{2}$ teaspoons salt
$\frac{1}{4}$ teaspoon white pepper
2 tablespoons flour
8 small boiled onions
4 oz button mushrooms, sautéed
$\frac{1}{2}$ cup cream
1 teaspoon lemon juice

Cut veal into neat 1-inch pieces and remove any bones. Melt 2 tablespoons butter in a heavy saucepan, add veal, raw onion and carrot and brown lightly. Add 1$\frac{1}{2}$ cups water, thyme, clove, parsley, bay leaf and seasoning. Bring gently to the boil and simmer for 1$\frac{1}{2}$-2 hours or until veal is tender. Strain off liquor, make up to 1$\frac{1}{2}$ cups with water and reserve. Remove veal and discard remaining ingredients. Melt remaining butter in a saucepan, add flour and cook a little. Pour in veal liquor, stirring constantly. When sauce boils add veal, small cooked onions and sautéed mushrooms. Simmer gently for 10 minutes, stirring occasionally. Add cream and lemon juice, adjust seasoning, heat through without boiling and serve hot.
TIME 1$\frac{3}{4}$-2$\frac{1}{4}$ hours.
GARNISH WITH bacon rolls, lemon butterflies and parsley sprigs.
SERVE WITH mashed or new potatoes and a crisp green vegetable.

ITALIAN VEAL AND MUSHROOMS

Serves 4
1 lb veal steak cut $\frac{1}{4}$-inch thick
2 tablespoons all-purpose flour
1 tablespoon olive oil
2 tablespoons butter or margarine
1 clove garlic, chopped
1 small onion, chopped
$\frac{1}{2}$ lb mushrooms, trimmed and sliced
$\frac{1}{2}$ cup white wine
1 teaspoon tomato paste
1 teaspoon salt
freshly ground black pepper
2 tablespoons light cream

Cut veal into 3-4 inch pieces and coat with flour. Brown in a frying pan (with lid) in hot oil and butter. Reduce heat and add garlic and onion and cook until onion is soft. Add mushrooms and cook a further 2 minutes. Add wine, tomato paste and seasoning. Cover and simmer for 30 minutes or until veal is tender. Stir in cream and serve immediately.
TIME 30 minutes.
GARNISH WITH sautéed mushrooms and chopped parsley.
SERVE WITH new, sautéed or mashed potatoes or pasta, a crisp green vegetable or a tossed salad.

VEAL MARENGO

Serves 4
1$\frac{1}{2}$ lb stewing veal
2 tablespoons flour
$\frac{1}{4}$ cup butter or margarine
2 tablespoons olive oil
2 onions, chopped
1 clove garlic, crushed
2 tablespoons tomato paste
1 cup veal stock (made from veal bones)
$\frac{1}{4}$ pint dry white wine
1$\frac{1}{2}$ teaspoons salt
freshly ground black pepper
1 thin strip orange peel
1 bay leaf
$\frac{1}{4}$ teaspoon dried thyme
4 oz button mushrooms or canned mushrooms

Cut veal into 1-inch cubes and toss in flour until well coated. Heat butter or margarine and oil in a heavy saucepan, add veal and brown on all sides (brown half veal, lift out, brown remainder). Remove veal and put aside, reduce heat, add onion and garlic to pan and sauté until onion is soft. Stir in tomato paste, stock and wine. Add salt, pepper, orange peel, bay leaf and thyme. Return veal to pan, cover and simmer for 1 hour. Add mushrooms and simmer for a further 30 minutes or until veal is tender. Remove orange rind and bay leaf before serving.
TIME 1$\frac{1}{2}$ hours.
GARNISH WITH chopped parsley.
SERVE WITH boiled rice, noodles, mashed or sautéed potatoes, a green vegetable or a tossed salad.

MEXICAN VEAL

Serves 4
1 breast of veal
3 tablespoons oil or ¼ cup butter
1 large onion, sliced
1 clove garlic
1 sweet red or green pepper, sliced in rings
½ cup skinned, chopped tomatoes
2 teaspoons chili powder
½ cup beef stock or water
salt
pepper (optional)

Cut breast of veal in 1-inch wide pieces. Brown breast of veal in hot oil or butter in a frying pan with lid. Reduce heat and sauté onion, garlic and pepper in covered pan until onion is soft. Add tomatoes, chili powder, stock or water and season to taste. Simmer, covered, for 1 hour or until veal is tender. Serve with the sauce spooned over the veal.
TIME 1 hour.
GARNISH WITH chopped parsley.
SERVE WITH boiled rice and a tossed salad.

VEAL PAPRIKA

Serves 4
1½ lb stewing veal
3 tablespoons oil
1 large onion, chopped
1 clove garlic, crushed
1½ teaspoons salt
freshly ground black pepper
1 tablespoon paprika
2 tablespoons chopped parsley
1½ cups beef stock or water
½ cup sour cream

Cut veal into 1-inch pieces. Heat oil in a heavy saucepan or flameproof casserole and brown veal quickly. Do this in two lots so that there will only be a single layer of veal in the pan each time. After the second lot has been removed, add onion and garlic, reduce heat and sauté until onion is soft. Return veal to pan and stir in salt, pepper, paprika and chopped parsley. Cook, stirring, for 2 minutes then add stock. Stir well to lift browned meat juices, bring to simmering point, cover tightly and simmer gently for 1¼-1½ hours or until veal is tender. Liquid should reduce to about ½ cup, if not, reduce it without lid to this amount. Stir in sour cream, heat without boiling and serve.
TIME 1¼-1½ hours.
GARNISH WITH chopped parsley.
SERVE WITH boiled noodles or rice, sauerkraut or a crisp green vegetable.

PAUPIETTES OF VEAL

Serves 4
4 veal steaks (boneless)
1 clove garlic
½ teaspoon salt
3 sage leaves or pinch of dried sage
4 thin slices ham
½ cup soft breadcrumbs
1 tablespoon all-purpose flour
oil for frying
½ cup white wine
½ cup skinned, chopped tomatoes
2 teaspoons tomato paste
salt
freshly ground black pepper to taste
½ teaspoon sugar

Flatten slices of veal with a meat pounder or a rolling pin and cut each in two. Crush garlic, mix with salt and chopped or rubbed sage leaves. Rub this into one side of each slice of veal. Place a slice of ham and a few breadcrumbs on each slice of veal. Roll veal up tightly and secure with wooden cocktail sticks. Coat each roll in flour and shallow fry in hot oil over a moderate heat until lightly browned on all sides. Add wine, tomatoes, tomato paste, salt, pepper and sugar. Cover tightly and simmer for 10-15 minutes or until veal is tender. Serve hot.
TIME 15 minutes.
GARNISH WITH chopped parsley.
SERVE WITH boiled rice and a tossed salad.

VEAL RAGOÛT

Serves 4
1½ lb stewing veal
¼ cup butter or margarine
1 onion, chopped
½ cup white wine
2 large, ripe tomatoes, skinned and chopped
1 large or 2 small sweet red peppers
salt
freshly ground black pepper
½ teaspoon sugar
chopped parsley

Trim and cut veal into neat 1-inch pieces. Heat butter or margarine in a heavy saucepan and brown veal. Add onions and cook until soft, stirring constantly. Pour in wine, cover and simmer 5 minutes. Add tomatoes, peppers cut in small strips and season to taste with salt and pepper and add sugar. Cover tightly and simmer for 1½ hours or until veal is tender. Serve hot sprinkled with chopped parsley.
TIME 1½ hours.
GARNISH WITH chopped parsley.
SERVE WITH boiled rice, mashed or sautéed potatoes and a green vegetable.

SALTIMBOCCA
Literally means 'jump in the mouth'

Serves 4
1 lb boneless veal leg steak, thinly cut
4 oz ham, thinly sliced
½ teaspoon dried sage or 8 fresh sage leaves
2 tablespoons butter or margarine
3 tablespoons white wine or marsala
3 tablespoons beef stock or water
½ teaspoon salt
freshly ground black pepper

Cut veal steak into 8 pieces. Place between two sheets of clear plastic and flatten with a rolling pin or the side of a meat pounder. Place a slice of ham, cut the same size as the veal, on each piece of steak. Place a sage leaf or a light sprinkling of dried sage on top of the ham. Roll up veal and ham and fasten rolls with wooden cocktail sticks. Brown rolls in butter on all sides in a frying pan which has a lid (about 10 minutes). Reduce heat and add wine or marsala and stock or water. Add salt and pepper, stir to lift pan juices, cover tightly and simmer very gently for 20 minutes, turning rolls occasionally, until veal is tender and liquor is reduced to a glaze. Serve immediately.
TIME 30 minutes.
GARNISH WITH chopped parsley.
SERVE WITH rice risotto and a tossed salad.

SWEET AND SOUR VEAL

Serves 4
1 lb stewing veal steak, ½-inch thick
2 onions
1 carrot
½ cup sliced celery
1 green pepper
2 tablespoons oil
1 x 1 lb can pineapple chunks
½ teaspoon ground ginger
1½ tablespoons vinegar
1½ tablespoons dry sherry
1½ tablespoons sugar
2 tablespoons soy sauce
1½ tablespoons cornstarch
salt and pepper

Cut veal into strips ¼-inch wide by 1½-inches long. Cut onion in half and slice lengthways. Slice carrot thinly, using a vegetable parer. Slice celery into ¼-inch slices, diagonally. Cut pepper into 1-inch long strips. Heat oil in a heavy pan and brown veal strips quickly over a high heat until sealed. Set aside and keep warm. Add more oil to pan if necessary and over lower heat, sauté prepared vegetables for 10 minutes. Add drained pineapple pieces, ginger, vinegar, sherry, sugar, soy sauce and ½ cup pineapple liquid. Cook a further 10 minutes. Mix cornstarch smoothly with remaining pineapple liquid, stir into sauce and bring to the boil to thicken the sauce. Add veal pieces, season to taste with salt and pepper and heat gently—do not boil. Serve hot.
TIME 25 minutes.
GARNISH WITH strips of green pepper.
SERVE WITH boiled or fried rice and a green vegetable if desired.

VEAL BIRDS

Serves 4
1½ lb veal leg steak, thinly cut
Herb and Bacon Stuffing (see page 75)
flour
1-2 tablespoons fat or oil
1 cup beef stock or water
1 teaspoon salt
freshly ground pepper
½ cup cream
1 tablespoon finely chopped parsley

Cut veal slices in half if large. Flatten veal between two pieces of plastic wrap with a meat cleaver or rolling pin. Spread stuffing on each piece of veal, roll up and fasten with toothpicks or tie with white string into neat rolls. Coat each 'bird' with flour and brown in a frying pan in fat or oil. Drain off excess fat and add stock, salt and pepper. Simmer, tightly covered, for 45 minutes-1 hour, or until veal is tender. Remove Veal Birds onto a hot serving dish and remove cocktail sticks or string. Reduce liquid in pan to about ¾ cup if necessary, stir in cream, adjust flavor and heat through without boiling. Pour over Veal Birds in dish. Sprinkle with finely chopped parsley and serve hot.
TIME 45-1 hour.
GARNISH WITH finely chopped parsley.
SERVE WITH boiled rice, mashed or duchesse potatoes and a green vegetable.

OSSO BUCCO

Serves 4
4 thick slices veal foreshank
1 teaspoon salt
freshly ground black pepper
2 tablespoons flour
2 tablespoons olive oil
¼ cup butter or margarine
1 clove garlic, chopped
1 onion, finely chopped
1 carrot, finely chopped
½ cup hot beef stock or water
½ cup dry, white wine
3 tablespoons tomato paste
1 bouquet garni
strip of lemon rind
3 tablespoons chopped parsley

Ask meat retailer to saw veal shanks into 3-inch pieces. Coat the slices of veal shank with the seasoned flour (mix salt and pepper with the flour). Heat oil and butter in a heavy, flameproof casserole or large heavy saucepan and brown veal on all sides. Add garlic, onion and carrot, reduce heat and cook until onion is soft. Add hot stock or water and wine, and tomato paste, bouquet garni and lemon rind. Bring to simmering point, cover and simmer gently for 1½ hours or until veal is tender (it should fall off the bones). Lift out bouquet garni and rind and discard. Serve Osso Bucco over saffron rice and sprinkle with chopped parsley.
TIME 1½ hours.
GARNISH WITH chopped parsley.
SERVE WITH rice and tossed salad.
NOTE the highlight of this dish is the marrow in the bones.

VEAL POT ROAST

Serves 4-6
1 shoulder of veal, boned
salt and pepper
2 tablespoons oil or fat
½ cup chopped onion
1 cup chopped carrot
½ cup chopped celery
1-2 cloves garlic, crushed
2 tablespoons flour
1 bay leaf
1 cup water
1 cup dry white wine

Open out shoulder of veal and season with salt and pepper. Roll up and tie into a neat roll with white string. Brown all over in hot oil or fat in a flameproof casserole or a deep, heavy saucepan. Lift out and keep aside. Reduce heat, add onion, carrot, celery and garlic. Sauté until onion is soft. Stir in flour. Cook, stirring, for 2 minutes, then add bay leaf, water and wine. Bring to the boil, reduce heat and return rolled veal to pan. If a saucepan is used, simmer gently for 1½ hours. If using a casserole it can be put into a moderately slow oven and cooked for the same time or until veal is tender. Remove veal to a hot serving dish, take off string, cover and keep warm. Strain sauce into another saucepan, pressing the vegetables through the sieve. Reduce sauce over a high heat to half its original quantity or until rather thick, spoon over the veal and serve.
TIME 1½ hours.
TEMPERATURE 325-350°F.
GARNISH WITH Sprigs of parsley.
SERVE WITH whole boiled potatoes, and braised root vegetables.

GROUND ESCALOPES OF VEAL

Serves 4
1 lb ground veal
1 small onion or 2 green onions, finely chopped
1 clove garlic, crushed
½ teaspoon grated lemon rind
2 tablespoons chopped parsley
1 egg
¼ cup dry breadcrumbs
1 teaspoon salt
¼ teaspoon pepper
flour for coating
1 egg beaten with 1 tablespoon water
extra dry breadcrumbs
oil for frying

Mix together minced veal, onion or green onions, garlic, lemon rind, parsley, egg, breadcrumbs and salt and pepper. Divide into eight pieces and shape each into a flat cake to resemble an escalope. Coat with flour, dip into beaten egg and then into breadcrumbs, pressing on firmly. Refrigerate for 30 minutes before shallow frying in hot oil over a moderate heat. Cook for 3-4 minutes on either side. Drain on absorbent paper and serve piping hot.
TIME 8 minutes.
GARNISH WITH lemon wedges and parsley sprigs.
SERVE WITH new or mashed potatoes, a green vegetable or tossed salad.

CHEESE VEAL SLICES

Serves 4
4·8 slices of left over roast veal
freshly ground black pepper
4 oz grated cheddar or gruyère (Swiss) cheese
1 teaspoon prepared mustard
1 tablespoon white wine
cream to mix

Cut veal ¼-inch thick. Place slices in a shallow baking dish and sprinkle with a little pepper, freshly ground for preference. Mix grated cheese, mustard and wine together and blend in enough cream to give a spreading consistency. Spread mixture over veal slices and when ready to serve, place under a preheated hot broiler and broil until sauce is golden (about 3 minutes). Serve immediately.
TIME 3 minutes.
GARNISH WITH chopped chives or parsley.
SERVE WITH new potatoes and a freshly cooked green vegetable or broiled tomatoes.

VEAL STUFFED PEPPERS

Serves 4
4 large green peppers
2 cups diced, leftover veal
2 tablespoons butter or margarine
¼ cup chopped onion
⅓ cup rice
1 x 1 lb can tomatoes
3 tablespoons tomato catsup
¼ cup beef stock or water
1 teaspoon worcestershire sauce
½ teaspoon dried basil
½ teaspoon dried thyme
2 tablespoons chopped parsley
salt and pepper
parmesan cheese

Cut tops from peppers, remove seeds and par-boil for 5 minutes. Place upside down on a rack to drain. Lightly and quickly brown veal in butter, remove from pan, leaving butter in pan, and put aside. Sauté onion in butter until soft, stir in rice, half tomatoes, 1 tablespoon tomato catsup stock or water, worcestershire sauce, herbs and season to taste. Cook, covered, until liquid is absorbed, stirring occasionally. Mix in veal and spoon into peppers Stand stuffed peppers in an ovenproof dish, sprinkle with parmesan cheese. Pour remaining tomatoes and tomato sauce into dish. Bake in a moderate oven for 30 minutes, adding a little water to dish if necessary. Serve immediately.
TIME 30 minutes.
TEMPERATURE 350-375°F.
GARNISH WITH parsley sprigs.
SERVE WITH boiled rice, French fried or mashed potatoes and a green vegetable.

LAMB

LAMB

SOME AMERICAN RETAIL CUTS

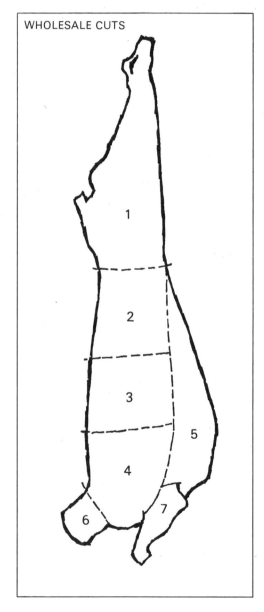

WHOLESALE CUTS

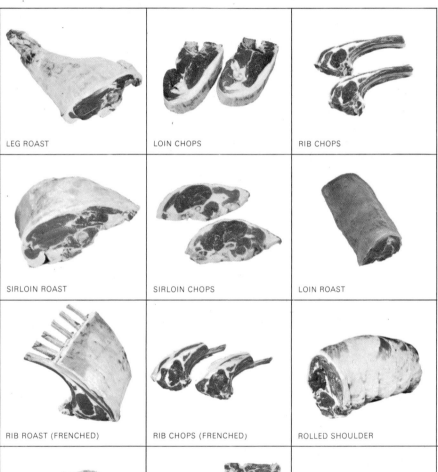

LEG ROAST	LOIN CHOPS	RIB CHOPS
SIRLOIN ROAST	SIRLOIN CHOPS	LOIN ROAST
RIB ROAST (FRENCHED)	RIB CHOPS (FRENCHED)	ROLLED SHOULDER

ROLLED BREAST (STUFFED)

BLADE CHOPS

ARM CHOP

SQUARE CUT SHOULDER

LEG STEAK

BASIC CUT	RETAIL CUT	COOKING METHOD
1 LEG	American Leg	Roast
	Frenched Leg	
	Sirloin Roast	
	Leg Steak	Broil, Pan-fry
	Sirloin Chops	Barbecue
2 LOIN	Loin Roast	Roast
	Rolled Loin	
	Loin Chops	Broil, pan-fry
	English Chops	Barbecue
3 RACK (also called Rib and Hotel Rack)	Rib Roast (Rack)	Roast
	Crown Roast	
	Rib Chops	Broil, pan-fry
	Rib Chops (Frenched)	Barbecue
4 SHOULDER	Square Cut Shoulder	Roast, Pot roast
	Rolled Shoulder	
	Shoulder (blade) chops	Broil, Pan-fry
	Shoulder (arm) Chops	Braise,
	Saratoga Chops	Barbecue
5 BREAST	Rolled Breast	Roast
	Breast	Braise
	Riblets	Braise, Cook in liquid
6 NECK	Neck Slices	Braise, cook in liquid
7 FORESHANK	Shanks	Braise, cook in liquid Barbecue if pre-tenderised

ROAST LEG OF LAMB

Serves 6-8
1 leg of lamb, about 6 lbs
freshly ground black pepper
salt

Wipe leg of lamb, weigh to calculate cooking time and place on a rack in a roasting pan. Rub fat surface with pepper and salt. Place a meat thermometer, if used, in center of flesh, making sure tip does not touch bone. Bake lamb in a moderately slow oven for calculated time. For underdone lamb, cook for 25 minutes per lb for well done lamb, add a further 25 minutes to the cooking time. If using a thermometer, roast to your own taste exactly. Basting is not required unless the lamb is very young with little fat coverage. Let the joint 'set' in a warm place for 15 minutes before carving.
TIME 25 minutes per lb plus 25 minutes extra.
TEMPERATURE 325-350°F.
GARNISH WITH roast potatoes and sprigs of parsley or mint.
SERVE WITH pan gravy (see page 72), mint sauce or mint jelly, baked squash or root vegetables (parsnip, carrot, onion) and a green vegetable.
VARIATION to make Crumbed Leg of Lamb, mix together 1 cup dry breadcrumbs, 3 tablespoons chopped parsley, 1 tablespoon lemon juice, a little salt and pepper. Bind with some dripping from the roast lamb. Baste roast 20 minutes before end of cooking time and press crumb mixture over surface. Return to oven and continue roasting for a further 20 minutes.

ROAST SHOULDER OF LAMB

Serves 6-8
1 shoulder of lamb (square cut or rolled)
1 clove garlic (optional)
juice of ½ lemon
salt
freshly ground black pepper
1 teaspoon rosemary spikes or ½ teaspoon dried, ground rosemary

Weigh shoulder and calculate cooking time. With a pointed knife, cut small slits in the meat surface of the shoulder of lamb. Cut clove of garlic into slivers and insert into slits. Omit this step if garlic is not used. Squeeze lemon juice over meat surface and sprinkle with salt, pepper and rosemary. Place lamb in a greased roasting pan, fat side up and cook in a moderately slow oven for calculated time, turn occasionally and baste during latter part of cooking time. Lift roast lamb out onto a carving platter and keep warm. Make gravy from pan juices (see page 72).
TIME 25-30 minutes per lb.
TEMPERATURE 325-350°F.
GARNISH WITH roast potatoes and sprigs of parsley or mint.
SERVE WITH pan gravy (see page 72) and mint sauce or mint jelly—roast vegetables and green peas.
WHAT TO DO WITH LEFTOVERS make into Shepard's Pie (see page 61) or Indian Parries (see page 61) or serve cold with salad or in sandwiches.

SEASONED BREASTS OF LAMB

Serves 4-6
2 breasts of lamb bones removed
lemon juice
salt and pepper
1-2 cloves garlic (optional)

Sausage Forcemeat:
12 oz sausage mince
½ cup soft breadcrumbs
2 tablespoons chopped parsley
2 tablespoons finely chopped onion

Trim excess fat from boned breasts of lamb. Place joints flat on working surface and sprinkle inside with lemon juice, salt and pepper. Spread Sausage Forcemeat on each breast. Roll up meat tightly and tie securely with white string or use metal skewers to hold together. If desired, make incisions in meat and insert slivers of garlic. Place on a rack in a roasting pan and cook in a moderate oven for 1-1½ hours. If any forcemeat remains, parboil some medium sized onions, remove centers and stuff with forcemeat. Bake onions with the meat for 30 minutes. Make gravy from pan juices (see page 72). To make sausage forcemeat, mix together sausage mince, breadcrumbs, parsley and onion. Season to taste.
TIME 1-1½ hours.
TEMPERATURE 325-350°F.
GARNISH WITH sprigs of mint leaves and stuffed onions.
SERVE WITH red currant jelly, roast potatoes and a spring green vegetable.

CROWN ROAST OF LAMB

Serves 6-8
1 crown roast of lamb (12-16 rib chops)
salt
freshly ground black pepper

The meat retailer will shape your crown roast from two racks or ribs, each containing 6-8 chops. If the lamb has a thick fat coverage, ask to have some of the fat trimmed off before shaping and sewing the crown roast.
To cook, place crown roast in a roasting pan—no rack is required—season with pepper, rub salt into fat surface only, and cover ends of bones with small pieces of aluminium foil to prevent them scorching. Roast in a moderate oven for 1¼-1½ hours, depending on size of chops. If desired, the center of the crown roast may be filled, before roasting, with a stuffing (see recipes pages 75-76). When the meat is cooked keep warm while making gravy (see page 72). Remove aluminium foil and place a paper frill on each bone. To serve, carve between chops. Alternatively, fill center after roasting with boiled small button onions in Béchamel Sauce (page 74) or freshly cooked green peas.
TIME 1¼-1½ hours.
TEMPERATURE 325-350°F.
GARNISH WITH root vegetables shaped into balls with a melon-ball scoop and roasted, mixed with boiled button onions and green peas—either in center or surrounding the crown roast.
SERVE WITH pan gravy (see page 72), mint sauce, roast potatoes and vegetable garnish.

GUARD-OF-HONOUR

Serves 4-6
2 racks of lamb, each with 6 rib chops—
frenched
salt and pepper
orange slices for garnish

Orange stuffing:
1 small onion, finely chopped
$\frac{1}{4}$ cup butter or margarine
2 cups (6 oz) soft breadcrumbs
1 tablespoon chopped parsley
grated rind and juice of 1 orange
salt and pepper
1 egg, beaten

Have butcher prepare Guard-of-Honour as for a Crown Roast, i.e. partly saw between the ribs for easier carving. Interlace racks of lamb to form an arch, fat side out, fasten together with string. Season surface fat with salt and pepper. Place in a greased roasting pan and fill center with Orange Stuffing. Bake in a moderate oven for 45 minutes-1$\frac{1}{4}$ hours, depending on size of lamb. Remove string, and place on warm platter.
To make Orange Stuffing, sauté onion in butter until soft. Mix into breadcrumbs with parsley, orange rind and juice and season to taste. Add enough beaten egg to bind stuffing together.
TIME 45 minutes-1$\frac{1}{4}$ hours.
TEMPERATURE 350-375°F.
GARNISH WITH slices of orange, sprigs of mint or parsley.
SERVE WITH gravy, roast potatoes and a green vegetable.

POT ROAST STUFFED SHOULDER OF LAMB

Serves 4-6
1 shoulder of lamb, bones removed
Herb and Bacon Stuffing (see page 75)
1 tablespoon flour
1$\frac{1}{2}$ teaspoons salt
freshly ground black pepper
2 tablespoons fat or butter
1 onion, quartered
2 carrots cut in chunky pieces
$\frac{1}{2}$ cup sliced celery
1 cup beef stock

Open out shoulder and spread with stuffing. Roll up and tie or sew securely with white string or linen thread. Mix flour with salt and pepper and rub into shoulder. Heat dripping or butter in a flameproof casserole or a heavy saucepan. Brown shoulder well on all sides over a moderate heat. Lift out meat and put aside, reduce heat and fry onion, carrot and celery until onion is soft and golden brown. Add stock, bring to the boil and return shoulder of lamb to pan. Cover and simmer gently, turning occasionally, for 2 hours or until meat is tender. Lift meat onto a heated serving platter, remove string or thread, pour some sauce over top and serve vegetables around shoulder. The sauce may be sieved, pressing the vegetables through into the sauce. Spoon some sauce over the shoulder of lamb and serve remainder separately.
TIME 2 hours.
GARNISH WITH sprigs of parsley.
SERVE WITH accompanying sauce, braised or boiled root vegetables, whole boiled potatoes and a green vegetable.

GRILLED CHOPS

Serves 4
4-8 lamb loin or sirloin chops cut
$\frac{3}{4}$-inch thick
salt and pepper

Trim chops of excess fat. Heat broiler until red hot and place chops on oiled rack 2-inches below the heat. Broil 1 minute on either side, then a further 5-7 minutes on either side, turning with tongs or two spoons. Season with salt and pepper and serve immediately with a pat of Parsley Butter (see Page 77) on each chop for added flavor.
TIME 12-16 minutes.
GARNISH WITH pats of parsley butter and a sprig of parsley.
SERVE WITH broiled tomatoes, new, mashed or French-fried potatoes and a green vegetable or tossed salad.
VARIATIONS
Marmalade Glazed Chops: Broil for required time on one side, turn, broil for 3-4 minutes on other side then top chops with a mixture of $\frac{1}{4}$ cup marmalade and 1 tablespoon lemon juice. Cook for a further 2 minutes. Season and serve immediately.
Herbed Chops: Before cooking, sprinkle each side of chops with lemon juice and oregano or rosemary. Season with salt and pepper after broiling.

CHEESE-TOPPED CHOPS

Serves 4-6
4 lamb loin chops cut 1-inch thick
salt and pepper

Cheese Topping:
2 tablespoons butter or margarine
2 tablespoons all-purpose flour
$\frac{1}{2}$ cup milk
1 small egg, beaten
1 small onion, grated
$\frac{1}{2}$ cup grated cheddar cheese
2 tablespoons Parmesan cheese
$\frac{1}{4}$ teaspoon salt
$\frac{1}{4}$ teaspoon pepper

Trim chops, and pan-broil over a moderate heat for 3 minutes on each side to seal in meat juices. Place in an ovenproof baking dish in a single layer and sprinkle with salt and pepper.
To make Cheese Topping, mix all ingredients together until evenly combined. Top each chop with cheese mixture, covering entire chop, and place in a moderate oven for 30 minutes. Serve immediately.
TIME 30-40 minutes.
TEMPERATURE 350-375°F.
GARNISH WITH a sprinkle of chopped parsley.
SERVE WITH baked tomatoes, mashed or new potatoes and a green vegetable.

NOISETTES OF LAMB

Serves 4
4 English or loin lamb chops or 4
lamb leg steaks
4 slices bacon, rind removed
melted butter or margarine
¼ lb small mushrooms, trimmed and
sliced
¼ cup butter or margarine
squeeze of lemon juice
4 croûtes, cut to size of lamb chops or
steaks
salt
freshly ground black pepper
1 tablespoon chopped parsley or
snipped chives

Trim off skin and most fat from lamb
and remove bone. Push each chop or
lamb steak into a round shape and wrap a
bacon rasher around each, securing with
toothpicks. Place meat on oiled broiler
rack under a preheated hot broiler and
broil 3-inches below heat for 6-8 minutes
on each side, cook a little longer for well
done meat. Brush top of noisettes (lamb
chops/steak) with butter during cooking.
Whilst noisettes are cooking, sauté mushrooms in 2 tablespoons butter with
lemon juice. Prepare croûtes by frying
circles of sliced bread in remaining
butter until crisp and golden. To serve,
place a noisette on each croûte on a
heated platter, season with salt and pepper and top with a spoonful of mushrooms and sprinkle with chopped parsley
or chives.
TIME 12-16 minutes.
GARNISH WITH sautéed mushrooms
and chopped parsley or snipped chives.
SERVE WITH mashed or sautéed potatoes and a green vegetable.

SOUVLAKIA
Greek Skewered Lamb

Serves 4
1½ lb boneless leg of lamb

Marinade:
1 onion, sliced
1 clove garlic, crushed
1½ teaspoons salt
freshly ground black pepper
2 bay leaves, each broken in 3 pieces
½ teaspoon dried marjoram
2 tablespoons oil
½ cup dry white wine

Trim excess fat from lamb and cut into
2-inch cubes. Place in a glass or earthenware bowl.
Combine ingredients for Marinade and
add to meat, mix well and refrigerate,
covered, for 8 hours, turning meat occasionally. When ready to broil lift lamb
out of marinade and thread meat onto
four skewers, adding a piece of bay leaf
between pieces of lamb as you fill the
skewers. Heat broiler until red hot and
place skewered lamb 3-inches below
heat. Broil for 15-20 minutes, turning
often and brush with marinade each time
the skewers are turned. Serve with boiled
rice or rice pilaff (cooked with onion,
green pepper and tomatoes).
TIME 15-20 minutes.
GARNISH WITH parsley sprigs and
lemon wedges.
SERVE WITH boiled rice or rice pilaff and
tossed salad or tomato salad.

PAN-FRIED LAMB STEAKS

Serves 4
4 lamb leg steaks
2 tablespoons butter or margarine
salt
freshly ground black pepper
parsley or watercress for garnish
Béarnaise Sauce or Garlic Butter for
serving

Remove bone from each chop, trim off
any excess fat and remove skin. Flatten
chops a little with the side of a meat
pounder. Melt butter in a heavy frying pan
and cook lamb steaks over a moderate
heat, browning well on each side (6
minutes in all). Place on a hot serving
platter, garnish with parsley or watercress and top each lamb steak with
Béarnaise Sauce (see page 74) or with a
pat of Garlic Butter (see page 77).
TIME 6 minutes.
GARNISH WITH sprigs of parsley or
watercress.
SERVE WITH creamed or new potatoes
and a green vegetable, or crusty French
bread and butter and a tossed salad.

CRUMBED RIB CHOPS

Serves 4
8 lamb frenched rib chops
lemon juice (optional)
salt and pepper
flour
1 egg, beaten with 1 tablespoon water
dry breadcrumbs
oil for frying

Trim skin and excess fat from chops,
flatten with the side of a meat pounder.
Lay chops on a plate, sprinkle with a
little lemon juice if desired and season
with salt and pepper. Stand in refrigerator for 1 hour. To finish chops coat with
flour then dip in beaten egg and finally
breadcrumbs, pressing them on firmly.
Heat oil, ¼-inch deep, in a heavy frying
pan over a moderate heat and fry the
chops for 4-5 minutes on either side.
Lift out, drain on absorbent paper and
serve immediately while crisp and piping
hot.
TIME 8-10 minutes.
GARNISH WITH chopped parsley.
SERVE WITH mashed potatoes, a green
vegetable or tossed salad.
VARIATIONS
Parsley Rib Chops: Add 2 tablespoons
finely chopped parsley to each ¼ cup
breadcrumbs.
Rib Chops Parmesan: To each ½ cup
breadcrumbs, add 2 tablespoons grated
Parmesan Cheese.
Rib Chops Rosemary: To each ½ cup
breadcrumbs add ¼ teaspoon powdered or
½ teaspoon dried spikes of rosemary.

LAMB STEW

Serves 4
1½ lb shoulder lamb chops
1 tablespoon all-purpose flour
1½ teaspoons salt
¼ teaspoon pepper
1 tablespoon oil or fat
1 onion, chopped
1 cup thickly sliced carrots
4 oz mushrooms, trimmed and sliced (optional)
1 cup beef stock or water
1 bay leaf, 2 sprigs parsley, 1 celery top, tied together
pinch of marjoram (optional)

Trim excess fat and any gristle from chops, and coat in seasoned flour. Heat oil or dripping in a heavy saucepan or flame-proof casserole and brown the chops, a single layer at a time, over a moderately high heat. Remove and put aside. Add onion and carrots to pan and sauté over a low heat. Add mushrooms, if used, and cook a few minutes longer. Add stock or water and stir well to lift any meat and flour on the bottom of pan. Add bouquet of flavoring herbs, return chops to pan, cover and simmer gently for 1¼-2 hours (depending on meat used) or until meat is tender. Stir occasionally. Lift out bouquet of flavoring herbs before serving. Serve Lamb Stew hot.
TIME 1¼-2 hours.
GARNISH WITH finely chopped parsley.
SERVE WITH boiled root vegetables, a green vegetable and boiled potatoes.
VARIATION if desired, 1 lb potatoes, cut in chunks, may be added to Lamb Stew 20 minutes before end of cooking time.

LAMB CHOPS CREOLE

Serves 4
1½ lb lamb sirloin chops
1 tablespoon oil
1 large onion, sliced
½ green pepper, sliced in strips
½ sweet red pepper, sliced in strips
1 clove garlic, chopped
½ cup skinned, chopped tomatoes or
½ cup canned tomatoes
2 tablespoons tomato catsup
1 teaspoon salt
freshly ground black pepper
½ teaspoon basil (optional)

Trim excess fat from chops. Fry chops in oil in a heavy frying pan until cooked through. Lift out of pan and keep hot on a hot serving dish. Place onion in pan and fry over a reduced heat until soft, add strips of pepper and garlic and cook for 5 minutes longer. Add tomatoes, tomato catsup, salt and pepper and basil, if used. Cover and simmer for 5 minutes. Pour creole sauce over chops and serve hot.
TIME 18-20 minutes.
GARNISH WITH a border of piped duchesse potatoes.
SERVE WITH mashed or duchesse potatoes and a crisp green vegetable.

APRICOT LAMB STEW—
Middle East Style

Serves 4
1½ lb boneless shoulder lamb
2 tablespoons oil
1 onion, chopped
1 teaspoon salt
freshly ground black pepper
¾ cup water
1 cup dried apricots
3 teaspoons sugar
3 tablespoons pine nuts, if available

Trim excess fat from lamb and cut into 2-inch cubes. Heat oil in a heavy pan or flameproof casserole and brown the meat on all sides, in two lots. Lift meat out and keep aside, reduce heat and sauté onion until soft. Return meat to pan and add salt, pepper and water. Cover and simmer for 45 minutes. Add apricots and sugar and simmer for a further 45 minutes, or until meat is tender. Add pine nuts, 5 minutes before end of cooking time. Serve Apricot Lamb Stew hot.
TIME 1½ hours.
GARNISH WITH sprigs of parsley.
SERVE WITH boiled rice and a green vegetable.
NOTE stir stew occasionally during later part of cooking as apricots tend to stick to pan. This is meant to be a thick stew.

CASSEROLE OF LAMB

Serves 4
1½ lb lamb shoulder chops
2 tablespoons flour
1½ teaspoons salt
¼ teaspoon pepper
2 tablespoons fat
1 large onion, chopped
1 green pepper, sliced
1 carrot, sliced
¼ cup sliced celery
2 tablespoons tomato paste
2 tablespoon tomato catsup
1 cup water

Trim chops and coat in seasoned flour. Brown chops in a fireproof casserole or a frying pan. Lift out and place aside or in a casserole if using a frying pan. Reduce heat and sauté onion until soft, add pepper, carrot and celery. Stir in tomato paste, tomato catsup and water. Return chops to fireproof casserole or pour vegetable mixture over chops if already in a casserole. Cook in a moderately slow oven for 1½-2 hours or until meat is tender. Serve Casserole of Lamb hot from casserole.
TIME 1½-2 hours.
TEMPERATURE 325-350°F.
GARNISH WITH chopped parsley.
SERVE WITH new, mashed or sautéed potatoes, boiled root vegetables and/or a green vegetable.

ARMENIAN LAMB

Serves 4
1½ lb boneless shoulder lamb
2 tablespoons oil
1 onion, sliced
2 cloves garlic, chopped
1 sweet red pepper, cut in chunks
1½ teaspoons salt
¼ teaspoon pepper
1 teaspoon ground coriander
1 cup beef stock or water
¼ cup yoghurt
1-2 teaspoons sugar

Trim excess fat from lamb and cut into 1-inch pieces. Heat oil in a heavy saucepan and sauté onion, garlic and pepper until soft. Add lamb, increase heat and stir until meat changes color, then continue cooking, stirring occasionally, until the meat juices evaporate and produce a brown sediment. Add salt and pepper, coriander, stock or water. Stir well to dissolve brown sediment of meat juices. Cover and simmer gently for 1-1¼ hours or until lamb is tender. The sauce should reduce during cooking, leaving a very thick stew. If the lamb is not tender at this stage add a little more liquid to prevent stew from burning. When cooked, stir in yoghurt and sugar according to taste. Serve Armenian Lamb hot.
TIME 1-1¼ hours.
GARNISH WITH chopped parsley and a border of piped mashed potato.
SERVE WITH extra mashed potato and peas or beans.

LAMB CURRY

Serves 4
1½ lb boneless lamb
2 tablespoons oil or ghee (clarified butter)
1 onion, chopped
1 clove garlic, crushed
1-2 tablespoons curry powder
½ green pepper, finely chopped
½ cup sliced celery
½ teaspoon ground ginger
¼ teaspoon paprika
½ cup coconut milk
½ cup beef stock or water
¼ cup seedless raisins
3 tablespoons yoghurt

Cut lamb into neat, small pieces and trim off any fat. Heat oil or ghee in a heavy saucepan and sauté meat, onion and garlic over a low heat. Stir in the curry powder and cook for 5 minutes then return meat to pan and cook for a further 10 minutes. Add pepper, celery, ginger, paprika, coconut milk (see page 23) stock or water and raisins. Stir well to blend, cover and simmer for 1½-2 hours or until meat is tender. Stir in yoghurt, heat through without boiling and serve with boiled rice.
TIME 1½-2 hours.
GARNISH WITH lemon and parsley sprigs and a border of boiled rice sprinkled with paprika.
SERVE WITH boiled rice, mango chutney, poppadums and a variety of Sambals (see page 94).

IRISH STEW

Serves 4
1½ lb shoulder lamb chops
2 tablespoons flour
1½ teaspoons salt
¼ teaspoon pepper
2 onions, sliced
1½ lb potatoes, thickly sliced
2 tablespoons chopped parsley

Trim chops and coat with flour seasoned with salt and pepper. Place a layer of sliced onions in base of an ovenproof casserole then cover with half the chops. Repeat layers, finishing with a layer of onions. Add cold water to just cover meat and onions. Place lid on casserole and cook in a moderately slow oven for 1¼ hours. Remove from oven and place potatoes on top of stew. Cook for a further 45 minutes. Serve hot sprinkled with chopped parsley.
TIME 2 hours.
TEMPERATURE 325-350°F.
GARNISH WITH finely chopped parsley.
SERVE WITH boiled root vegetables and a green vegetable.

NAVARIN OF LAMB

Serves 4
2½ lb boneless shoulder or leg of lamb
¼ cup butter or margarine
1 onion, quartered
1 clove garlic, crushed
2 tablespoons flour
½ teaspoon sugar
1½ teaspoons salt
freshly ground black pepper
1 cup beef stock or water
3 tablespoons tomato paste
½ teaspoon dried thyme
1 celery stalk with leaves
1 bay leaf
1 turnip, halved and thickly sliced
8 small onions
8 small potatoes
1 cup fresh, shelled peas
2 tablespoons chopped parsley

Trim excess fat from meat and cut into 1½-inch cubes. Fry meat in butter with quartered onion until browned. Add garlic, flour and sugar. Cook, stirring, until flour is colored a little. Add seasoning, stock or water, tomato paste, thyme, celery leaves and bay leaf. Place in a casserole, add turnip and cook, covered, in a moderate oven for 1 hour. Remove celery and bay leaf, add remaining vegetables and cook for a further 1½ hours or until meat is tender.
TIME 2½ hours.
TEMPERATURE 350-375°F.
GARNISH WITH chopped parsley.
SERVE WITH a green vegetable if desired.

MARINATED CHOPS WITH MUSHROOMS

Serves 4
1½ lb lamb shoulder chops
1 tablespoon butter or margarine
¼ lb mushrooms, trimmed and sliced

Marinade:
¾ cup dry white wine
1 onion, chopped
1 clove garlic, chopped
½ teaspoon dried marjoram
½ teaspoon dried thyme
½ teaspoon sugar
salt and freshly ground black pepper
2 tablespoons oil

Trim excess fat from chops and place in a glass or earthenware dish. Mix marinade ingredients together, pour over chops, cover and leave in refrigerator for at least 8 hours. Too cook, lift chops out of marinade and fry in a frying pan (with lid) until browned on each side. Pan should need no fat at this stage as oil in marinade coats the chops. Lift chops out when browned. Pour marinade through a strainer, reserve liquid and add onions to pan. Sauté onions over a low heat until soft, add butter and sliced mushrooms and cook a little longer. Add liquid from marinade, bring to boil, return chops to pan and cover. Simmer gently for 45 minutes or until chops are tender. Sauce should be reduced but thicken with corn-starch if desired. Serve hot.
TIME 45 minutes.
GARNISH WITH chopped parsley.
SERVE WITH boiled rice or mashed potatoes and a green vegetable.

MOUSSAKA

Serves 4-6
1½ lb ground lean lamb
oil for frying
1 large onion, chopped
2 cloves garlic, chopped
1 cup skinned, chopped tomatoes
2 tablespoons tomato paste
1 bay leaf
1 small onion studded with 3 cloves
1½ teaspoons salt
freshly ground black pepper
1 teaspoon sugar
2 large eggplant (aubergine)
flour
2 cups Cheese Sauce (see page 72)

Brown ground lamb in oil in a heavy saucepan, reduce heat, add onion and garlic. Cook until onion is soft. Add tomatoes, tomato paste, bay leaf, clove-studded onion, salt and pepper, sugar and ½ cup water. Cover and simmer for 30 minutes or until sauce is thick. Cut eggplant into ¼-inch slices, soak in water for 30 minutes. Drain and dry with paper towels. Coat eggplant with flour, fry until golden in ¼-inch hot oil. Drain and arrange a layer of eggplant in the base of a rectangular ovenproof dish (8 x 12-inches and 2-3-inches deep). Top with half the lamb mixture, repeat layers, finishing with a layer of eggplant.
Pour Cheese Sauce over top and sprinkle with extra grated cheese. Bake in a moderate oven for 30 minutes.
TIME 30 minutes.
TEMPERATURE 350-375°F.
GARNISH WITH slices of grilled tomato or chopped parsley.
SERVE WITH a green vegetable or salad.

RAGOÛT OF LAMB

Serves 4
1½ lb boneless lamb
¼ lb thick bacon slices
1 tablespoon oil
1 large onion, sliced
1 clove garlic, chopped
1½ tablespoons salt
freshly ground black pepper
½ teaspoon marjoram
½ teaspoon dried rosemary spikes or
¼ teaspoon ground rosemary
3 tablespoons tomato paste
¼ cup dry red wine
1 cup beef stock or water

Trim excess fat from lamb and cut into 1-inch cubes. Chop bacon, place in pan in which ragoût is to be cooked and cover with water. Bring to the boil, drain off water, return to heat with 1 tablespoon oil added and fry bacon until crisp. Drain and put aside. Brown lamb in oil and fat mixture in pan, lift out. Add onion and garlic to pan and sauté until soft over a low heat, add seasoning, herbs, tomato paste, wine and stock. Stir well and return bacon and lamb to pan. Cover and simmer for 1 hour or until lamb is tender. Sauce should be thick enough at the end of this time. Serve hot.
TIME 1 hour.
GARNISH WITH chopped parsley and sliced tomato.
SERVE WITH new, mashed or sautéed potatoes and a green vegetable or a tossed salad.

SPICY LAMB RIBLETS IN BARBECUE SAUCE

Serves 4-6
2 lb lamb riblets
1 large onion, chopped
1 clove garlic, chopped
½ cup tomato sauce
¼ cup cider or wine vinegar
1 tablespoon worcestershire sauce
2 tablespoons chutney
1 tablespoon brown sugar
1½ teaspoons salt
freshly ground black pepper
¾ cup water
Trim off excess fat from riblets. Heat a frying pan and place in riblets, fat side down. Brown well on all sides pouring off fat as it accumulates. Lift meat out when well browned and keep aside. Sauté onion and garlic in a little fat until soft, add tomato sauce, cider or wine vinegar, worcestershire sauce, chutney, brown sugar, salt and pepper. Stir in water and return riblets to pan. Simmer over a low heat, covered, for 45 minutes-1 hour or until meat is tender adding a little more water if necessary towards end of cooking time if sauce reduces too much. Check seasoning skim off fat and serve piping hot.
TIME 45 minutes-1 hour.
GARNISH WITH chopped parsley or chives.
SERVE WITH jacket baked potatoes and butter or boiled rice and a green vegetable or tossed salad.

LAMB AND VEGETABLE CASSEROLE

Serves 4-6
1½ lb shoulder lamb chops
1 tablespoon flour
1½ teaspoons salt
freshly ground black pepper
1 tablespoon oil or fat
1 large onion, sliced
1 clove garlic, crushed
1 green and 1 sweet red pepper, sliced
2 tablespoons tomato paste
1 cup beef stock or water
½ lb zucchini (courgettes), sliced
1 cup fresh, shelled peas
chopped parsley for garnish

Trim chops, removing excess fat and any gristle. Coat chops with seasoned flour and brown over a high heat in a heavy frying pan in hot oil or fat. Lift meat out and place it directly into an ovenproof casserole. Add onion and garlic to pan and over a reduced heat, sauté the onion until soft. Add sliced pepper, sauté for 1-2 minutes, then add tomato paste, chopped tomatoes and stock. Return chops to flameproof casserole or pour liquid over chops if using an ovenproof casserole. Cover and cook in a moderate oven for 2 hours. Thirty minutes before end of cooking time add sliced zucchini and green peas. Serve, sprinkled with chopped parsley, from the casserole at the table.
TIME 2 hours.
TEMPERATURE 350-375°F.
GARNISH WITH chopped parsley.
SERVE WITH baked jacket potatoes and a tossed salad.

GREEK LAMB AND MACARONI BAKE

Serves 4
1 lb boneless lamb
¼ cup butter or oil
1½ teaspoons salt
¼ teaspoon pepper
1 onion, chopped
1 clove garlic, crushed
1 cup skinned, chopped tomatoes
2 tablespoons tomato paste
2 cups hot beef stock
1 bay leaf
2 cloves
1 teaspoon sugar
8 oz macaroni
4 oz gruyère or cheddar cheese, diced

Trim fat from lamb and cut into 1-inch cubes. Place in a casserole, dot with butter or sprinkle with oil, season with salt and pepper and cook in a hot oven for 15 minutes. Add onion and garlic and cook a further 10 minutes. Remove from oven and stir in tomatoes and tomato paste mixed with stock. Add bay leaf, cloves and sugar. Cover and replace in oven. Reduce temperature to moderate and cook for 30 minutes. Stir in macaroni and 1 cup water and cook covered for a further 45 minutes or until macaroni is tender. Stir occasionally during cooking. Remove foil, sprinkle cheese over, return to oven for 10 minutes to melt cheese. Serve at the table from the dish.
TIME 1½-2 hours.
TEMPERATURE 400-450°F reducing to 350-375°F.
GARNISH WITH broiled tomato slices.
SERVE WITH a tossed green salad.

BRAISED LAMB SHANKS

Serves 4
4 lamb fore shanks
2 tablespoons fat or oil
1 onion, chopped
1 clove garlic (optional)
1 carrot, diced
½ cup diced celery
1 cup skinned, chopped tomatoes or canned tomatoes
1 teaspoon salt
¼ teaspoon pepper
½ teaspoon sugar
¼ cup beef stock or water
1 teaspoon worcestershire sauce

Brown lamb shanks in hot fat or oil in a frying pan (with lid) over a moderately high heat. Pour off all but a little of the fat and reduce heat. Add onion, garlic if used, carrot and celery and cook until onion is soft. Stir in tomatoes, salt, pepper, sugar, stock or water and worcestershire sauce. Spoon some of the vegetable mixture over the shanks, cover and simmer for 1½-2 hours or until tender. It may be necessary to add a little more liquid to the pan during cooking Check flavor before serving.
TIME 1½-2 hours.
GARNISH WITH chopped parsley.
SERVE WITH mashed potatoes or boiled rice and a green vegetable.

CORNISH PASTIES

Serves 4
1 lb stewing lamb
1 tablespoon fat
1 onion, chopped
½ pint beef stock
salt and pepper
1 cup diced potato, par-boiled
2 tablespoons chopped parsley
Plain Pastry

Trim and cut meat into ½-inch cubes, fry until browned in hot fat. Add onion and cook 5 minutes over a low heat. Add stock, salt and pepper. Simmer, covered, for 1 hour or until meat is tender, then stir in potato and parsley. Leave to cool.
Plain Pastry; Follow recipe as given on page 75, but make double quantity. Roll out ⅛-inch thick, cut into 5-inch rounds, using a saucepan lid or saucer as a guide. Turn rounds of pastry over, place a heaped tablespoon of the cold meat mixture in the center of each and moisten edges with cold water. Bring edges of pastry together and press together to seal. Roll edges over in overlapping fashion or flute with fingers. Place pasties upright on a greased baking tray. Brush with beaten egg or milk and bake in a hot oven for 10 minutes, reduce heat to moderate and bake for a further 10-15 minutes.
TIME 1 hour for meat filling. 20-25 minutes for Cornish Pasties.
TEMPERATURE 400-450°F reducing to 350-375°F.
GARNISH WITH sprigs of parsley.
SERVE WITH mashed potatoes and a green vegetable when hot or serve cold for a packed lunch or picnic.

COLONIAL GOOSE

Serves 4-6
1 rolled shoulder of lamb
salt and pepper
2 large onions, finely chopped
1½ cups chopped carrot
1 tablespoon oil
1 tablespoon oil
½ cup water
1 cup red wine
2 tablespoons parsley
½ teaspoon dried thyme or
1 teaspoon fresh chopped thyme
Herb and Bacon Stuffing (see page 75)

Open out shoulder of lamb. Season with salt and pepper and spread with stuffing. Roll up and tie into a roll with white string. Weigh meat and calculate cooking time (35 minutes per lb). Place in a heated casserole and cook until brown. Lift out, add oil to pan and sauté onion and carrot until onion is soft. Add water and red wine. Place meat on top of vegetables, add parsley and thyme and cover. Simmer for calculated time, turning occasionally. Test flavour and adjust seasoning if necessary. When meat is tender lift onto a serving dish, remove string and keep warm. Sieve liquid and vegetables to make a sauce. Serve Mock Goose hot with sauce.
TIME 2½-3 hours.
GARNISH WITH sprigs of parsley.
SERVE WITH boiled potatoes and a green vegetable.

SWEDISH COFFEE-BASTED LAMB

Serves 6
1 rolled shoulder of lamb
salt and pepper
1 cup strong coffee
¼ cup light cream
2 teaspoons sugar
2 tablespoons flour
water
2 tablespoons red currant jelly

Wipe lamb and weigh to calculate cooking time. Place in a roasting pan (without rack) and rub salt and pepper into fat surface. Bake in a moderately slow oven for 30 minutes per lb. After 1 hour add coffee mixed with cream and sugar to pan and baste lamb occasionally during remainder of cooking time. Lift out lamb and rest in a warm place before carving. Place 2 tablespoons fat from pan drippings into a saucepan. Skim off remaining fat in pan and add sufficient water to pan to make 1½ cups with juices. Heat fat in saucepan and stir in flour. Cook 1 minute. Pour in dissolved juices, stirring constantly until gravy boils and thickens. Stir in the red currant jelly and heat until melted. Serve with the lamb.
TIME 30 minutes per lb.
TEMPERATURE 325°-350°F.
GARNISH WITH parsley sprigs.
SERVE WITH roast potatoes and onions, baked squash and a green vegetable.
NOTE: A leg of lamb may be cooked in the same way.

BOILED LEG OF LAMB WITH CAPER SAUCE

Serves 4-6
½ leg of lamb
4 carrots
4 small turnips
4 onions
1 tablespoon salt
½ tablespoon pepper

Caper Sauce:
¼ cup butter or margarine
2 tablespoons all-purpose flour
1½ cups liquid from lamb
salt
pinch of cayenne pepper
¼ cup drained capers

Wipe leg of lamb. Bring sufficient water to cover lamb to the boil in a large, heavy saucepan. Plunge leg into water, add vegetables, bring to a slow boil and boil for 10 minutes before adding salt and pepper. Cover, reduce heat and simmer for 2-2½ hours or until meat is tender. Skim off fat and leave leg in liquid whilst making Caper Sauce. Serve boiled lamb surrounded with vegetables and accompanied with Caper Sauce.
To make Caper Sauce, melt butter in a saucepan, stir in flour, cook for 2 minutes over a medium heat. Pour in hot liquid off the heat, stirring in a little at a time. Return to heat, bring to the boil stirring continusouly. Season with salt and cayenne pepper and stir in capers.
TIME 2-2½ hours.
GARNISH WITH Caper Sauce poured over lamb and parsley sprigs.
SERVE WITH boiled root vegetables and boiled potatoes.

HERBED ROSETTES OF LAMB

Serves 4
2 lb lamb neck slices (rosettes)
¼ cup butter or 4 tablespoons fat
salt
freshly ground black pepper
2 tablespoons lemon juice
1 teaspoon prepared mustard
2 tablespoons chopped parsley
1 teaspoon dried sweet basil

Trim chops and brown on each side in hot butter or fat in a frying pan (with lid). Season meat with salt and pepper. Combine lemon juice, mustard, parsley and basil. Spoon over chops (chops should be in a single layer), cover and cook over low heat until meat is tender, about 1 hour. Turn chops halfway through cooking time.
TIME 1 hour.
GARNISH WITH chopped parsley.
SERVE WITH boiled rice or new, mashed or sautéed potatoes and a green vegetable.
NOTE shoulder chops may be cooked in the same way.

MOUSSAKA
(using leftover lamb)

Serves 4
2 cups finely diced roast lamb
¼ cup butter
1 onion, chopped
4 oz mushrooms, trimmed and sliced
1 cup skinned, chopped tomatoes
1 tablespoon tomato catsup
¼ cup beef stock
salt and pepper
2 tablespoons chopped parsley
1 large eggplant, sliced
oil for frying
grated cheddar cheese

Fry diced lamb quickly in melted butter in a heavy saucepan, stirring constantly. Lift out and keep aside. Add onion to pan and fry over a low heat until soft. Add mushrooms and stir until cooked. Add tomatoes, tomato sauce, stock, seasoning and parsley. Cover and cook for 10 minutes. Return meat to pan and simmer gently, covered, for 10 minutes (do not boil).
While sauce is cooking, fry sliced eggplant in oil ¼-inch deep in a frying pan, until browned on both sides. Drain on absorbent paper.
Line an ovenproof casserole with eggplant slices, top with lamb and tomato mixture. Sprinkle liberally with cheese and place under a hot grill until cheese is golden brown.
TIME 25-30 minutes.
GARNISH WITH grilled cheese and chopped parsley.
SERVE WITH boiled rice and a crisp green vegetable or tossed salad.

INDIAN PATTIES

Serves 4
2 cups ground, cooked lamb
1 small onion, finely chopped
1 egg
3 tablespoons chutney
2 teaspoons curry powder
1 teaspoon salt
½ cup boiled rice
flour
egg for coating
dry breadcrumbs
oil for shallow frying

Mix together ground lamb, onion, beaten egg, chutney, curry powder, salt and rice until well blended. Take a heaped tablespoon of the mixture at a time and shape and flatten into cutlet shapes with moistened hands. Coat with flour, then brush with beaten egg and coat with breadcrumbs, pressing them on firmly. An egg slice or a palette knife will help you in handling the patties. Shallow fry the patties in hot oil over a moderate heat for 2 minutes on either side. Serve piping hot.
TIME 4 minutes.
GARNISH WITH lemon wedges and parsley sprigs.
SERVE WITH boiled rice, fruit chutney and a freshly cooked green vegetable.

SWEET LAMB CURRY

Serves 4
2 cups diced roast lamb
2 tablespoons butter
1 onion, chopped
1 green apple, peeled and chopped
1 tablespoon curry powder
1 teaspoon salt
1 cup beef stock
2 teaspoons sugar
2 tablespoons sultanas or raisins
1 tablespoon lemon juice

Trim off any fat and gristle from lamb before dicing and measuring. Melt butter in a heavy saucepan and sauté onion until soft. Add apple and curry powder and cook for 3 minutes, stirring constantly. Add salt, stock, sugar, sultanas or raisins and simmer for 15 minutes. Stir in lamb, cover and simmer very gently (do not boil) for 10 minutes. Stir in lemon juice and serve hot.
TIME 25 minutes.
GARNISH WITH lemon twists and parsley sprigs and surround with a border of boiled rice sprinkled with paprika.
SERVE WITH boiled rice and fresh green peas, fruit chutney and various sambals (see page 95).

SHEPHERD'S PIE

Serves 4
1 lb cooked roast lamb
2 tablespoons butter
1 onion, finely chopped
1 clove garlic (optional)
1 stalk celery
1 tablespoon flour
½ cup leftover lamb gravy
½ cup beef stock or use
1 cup gravy
2 tablespoons chopped parsley
salt and pepper
1 lb potatoes, boiled and mashed
2 tablespoons butter

Trim fat and gristle from lamb and cut into small cubes. Melt butter in a heavy saucepan and sauté onion, garlic and celery over a low heat for 10 minutes. Stir in flour and cook until it is light gold in color. Blend in gravy and stock and cook until bubbling. Add lamb and parsley and remove from heat. Season to taste with salt and pepper.
Line sides of a deep pie dish with a layer of mashed potatoes, add lamb mixture, spread remaining potatoes on top, smooth with a knife, decorate with a fork and dot with butter. Cook in a moderate oven for 30 minutes or until potato is browned. Serve hot.
TIME 30 minutes.
TEMPERATURE 350-375°F.
GARNISH WITH a sprig of parsley.
SERVE WITH a freshly cooked green vegetable and boiled carrots or squash.
NOTE the shelf above the center shelf is the best position for browning.

CARVING

LEG OF LAMB: This method is simple, and gives a high yield of sliced meat. Wrap a cloth or napkin around the bone or 'handle' of the leg. Hold the leg by the handle and rest on a carving plate at an angle of 45°, the meatiest side uppermost. Starting midway on the joint, slice the meat down at an oblique angle. Slice down again at an opposite oblique angle and remove the wedge shaped piece of meat. Continue slicing down each side of the cut. Slices should be about $\frac{1}{8}$-inch thick. Keep slicing until the leg bone is reached. Turn the leg over and repeat the process.

PORK LOIN ROAST: Ask your meat retailer to saw free the backbone from the rib. After roasting remove backbone and place roast with the bone side facing the carver.
Place fork in the top of the roast. Slice by cutting along each side of the rib bone. One slice will contain the rib and the next will be boneless.

HAM: Place ham on carving plate with the shank bone at the carver's left. Begin by removing a small wedge from the shank end. Cut even, thin slices down to the bone. Then thin slices may be carved from the butt end after which the ham may be turned over and carved from the other side.

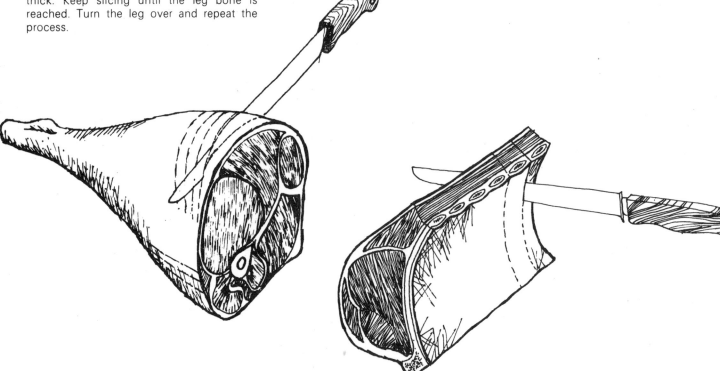

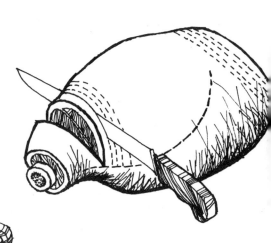

RIB OF BEEF: Place the roast on carving board with ribs to left. Place fork between 2 ribs to hold firmly. Slice from right (fat) edge towards ribs. With point of knife loosen slice from rib bone and remove to warm plate.

ROLLED RIB AND ROLLED RUMP OF BEEF:

Method 1—Using a fork with a safety guard, hold the joint flat on the carving plate. Slice meat across the grain towards the fork.

Method 2—Hold the joint on its side with a fork. Slice downwards towards the carving plate.

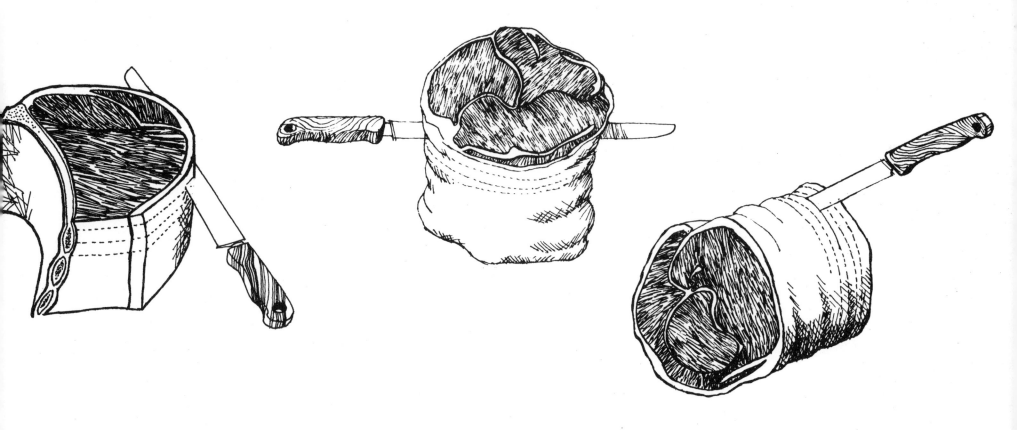

VARIETY MEATS

CRUMBED BRAINS AND BACON
FRICASSÉED BRAINS
SCRAMBLED BRAINS AND
 EGGS
STUFFED ROAST HEARTS
DEVILLED KIDNEYS
FRIED LIVER AND BACON   A
BEEF KIDNEY STEW
FRIED LIVER PIQUANT
BAKED LIVER AND ONIONS
CHOPPED LIVER AND EGGS
LIVER PÂTÉ   C
CREAMED SWEETBREADS   B
SAUTÉED SWEETBREADS
LAMBS' TONGUES WITH
 RAISIN SAUCE
TRIPE AND ONIONS
BOILED BEEF TONGUE

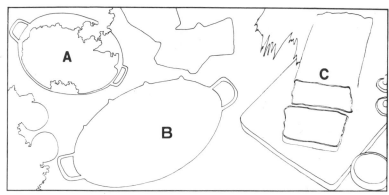

CRUMBED BRAINS AND BACON

Serves 4
1½ lb lamb's or calf's brains
1 small onion, halved
    (optional)
1 tablespoon vinegar
2 tablespoons all-purpose flour
2 teaspoons salt
½ teaspoon pepper
1 egg, beaten with 1 tablespoon water
dry breadcrumbs
oil for frying
¼ lb sliced bacon, rind removed

Remove skin from brains under running cold water. Place in a saucepan and cover with cold water. Add onion, if used, vinegar and 1 teaspoon salt and bring to simmering point. Allow to simmer gently for 20 minutes. Lift brains out, drain and allow to cool. Slice brains and pat dry. Mix flour with salt and pepper and coat each piece of brain. Dip in egg and coat with breadcrumbs, pressing them on firmly. Place enough oil in a frying pan to cover base about ¼-inch in depth. Heat and fry brains until golden on all sides. Cut bacon slices in half, roll and place on skewers. Broil until cooked. Place brains on a heated serving platter and garnish with bacon rolls.
TIME 10 minutes.
GARNISH WITH lemon wedges and parsley sprigs.
SERVE WITH broiled tomatoes.

FRICASSÉED BRAINS

Serves 4
1½ lb lamb's or calf's brains
1 onion, halved
1 tablespoon vinegar
1 teaspoon salt
1 cup Béchamel Sauce (see page 74)
12 small button onions, boiled
¼ lb button mushrooms, trimmed and
    sautéed in butter and lemon juice
salt and pepper

Wash and remove skin from brains under running cold water. Place in a saucepan with onion, cover with water, add vinegar and salt and bring to simmering point. Simmer for 20 minutes. Drain, cut in small piece and place in Béchamel Sauce. Add prepared onions and mushrooms, taste and adjust seasoning. Heat through gently without boiling and serve on a heated dish.
TIME 25 minutes.
GARNISH WITH triangles of toast and chopped parsley.
SERVE WITH bacon rolls, sautéed potatoes if desired, and a crisp green vegetable.

SCRAMBLED BRAINS AND EGGS

Serves 4
1 lb brains, lamb's or calf's
1 small onion, sliced
1 tablespoon vinegar
4 eggs
2 teaspoons salt
3 tablespoons milk
1 tablespoon tomato catsup
1 teaspoon worcestershire sauce
¼ cup butter
1 tablespoon chopped parsley

Wash and skin brains under running cold water. Place in a saucepan with onion, cover with cold water, add vinegar and 1 teaspoon salt, and bring to a slow boil. Reduce heat and simmer for 20 minutes. Drain, and when cool, break into ½-inch pieces.
Beat the eggs slightly, add remaining salt, milk and sauces. Stir in brains. Heat the butter in a frying pan over a medium heat, taking care not to burn it. Pour on the seasoned eggs and brains and scramble as for scrambled eggs. Serve hot sprinkled with chopped parsley.
TIME 10 minutes.
GARNISH WITH chopped parsley.
SERVE WITH buttered toast.

STUFFED ROAST HEARTS

Serves 4
4-8 veal or lamb hearts, according to size
Sage and Onion Stuffing (see page 75)
2-3 tablespoons fat
salt and pepper

Wash hearts thoroughly in cold water. Cut off flaps and lobes and remove all pieces of gristle. Cut away the membrane which divides the two cavities and check that the inside is free of blood. Soak hearts in cold water for 30 minutes, drain and dry.
Fill hearts with stuffing and sew each one with thick thread. Place in a roasting pan and spread fat on top. Bake in a moderately slow oven for 1-1½ hours or until tender. Turn during cooking. Serve either whole or carved into slices.
TIME 1-1½ hours.
TEMPERATURE 325-350°F.
GARNISH WITH parsley sprigs and baked tomatoes.
SERVE WITH pan gravy (see page 72), roast potatoes and green vegetables.

BOILED BEEF TONGUE

Serves 6-8
1 beef tongue, fresh or pickled
1 tablespoon salt (for fresh tongue)
4 whole cloves
3 peppercorns
1 tablespoon vinegar
1 stalk celery

Scrub the beef tongue under running cold water. If salted tongue, soak in cold water for 2 hours after scrubbing and drain well.
Place tongue in a deep kettle, add salt, cloves, peppercorns, vinegar and celery and cover with cold water, cover pan and bring to a slow boil. Simmer for 3 hours over a gentle heat or until tender (test with a skewer, which should penetrate to the center easily). Allow tongue to stand in cooking liquid until cool enough to handle. Lift out and pull off outer skin. Remove any bones and gristle from root. Serve tongue sliced.
TIME 3 hours for cooking. 2 hours for soaking a salted tongue.
GARNISH WITH parsley sprigs or watercress.
SERVE WITH Horseradish Sauce (see page 77) pickled beet salad and tossed salad, or serve in sandwiches.

DEVILLED KIDNEYS

Serves 4
6 lamb kidneys
1 tablespoon tomato catsup
1 teaspoon worcestershire sauce
½ teaspoon dry mustard
2 tablespoons soft butter
1 teaspoon chutney
2 teaspoons lemon juice
½ teaspoon salt
freshly ground black pepper
4 slices of toast
chopped parsley

Wash and skin kidneys. Cut in half and remove core. Slice each half in two giving thin slices. Place in a greased baking dish or bottom part of broiler. Mix together sauces, mustard, butter, chutney, lemon juice and seasoning. Spread over sliced kidney and broil for 8-10 minutes, turning once. Serve Devilled Kidneys on toast with sauce spooned over.
TIME 8-10 minutes.
GARNISH WITH
SERVE WITH buttered toast.
NOTE a popular breakfast dish.

FRIED LIVER AND BACON

Serves 4
1 lb veal or lamb liver
¼ lb bacon slices
seasoned flour

Buy liver in ½-inch slices. Dry with paper towels and coat with seasoned flour (2 tablespoons flour mixed with ½ teaspoon salt and ¼ teaspoon pepper).
Place bacon slices in a heated frying pan and cook until done to your liking. Lift out and keep warm. If insufficient bacon fat in pan, add a little lard or fat. Fry liver over a moderately high heat for 5 minutes on either side, or until tender. Lift out onto a serving platter and serve with bacon slices.
TIME 12-15 minutes.
GARNISH WITH sprig of parsley.
SERVE WITH mashed potatoes, fried tomatoes and a green vegetable.

BEEF KIDNEY STEW

Serves 4
1 beef kidney (1¼-1½ lb)
1 tablespoon flour
2 slices bacon, finely chopped
2 tablespoons fat or butter
½ cup sliced celery
1 large onion, chopped
1 cup canned tomatoes or fresh chopped tomatoes
1 green pepper, chopped
1 teaspoon salt
freshly ground black pepper
½ cup beef stock or water

Wash kidney and par-boil in salted water for 15 minutes to remove alkaline odours. Remove kidney, rinse well and drain. Cut kidney in half, remove fat and tubes. Cut kidney into ½-inch slices and coat with flour. Chop bacon slices finely and fry gently in a pan until lightly colored. Add fat and brown kidney pieces with bacon. Add celery and onions and cook, stirring, until onion is soft. Add tomatoes, pepper, salt and pepper and stock. Stir well, cover and simmer for 30-45 minutes or until kidney is tender and serve hot.
TIME 30-45 minutes.
GARNISH WITH chopped parsley.
SERVE WITH boiled rice or macaroni noodles and carrots or a green vegetable.

FRIED LIVER PIQUANT

Serves 4
veal or lamb liver
salt
2 tablespoons flour
freshly ground black pepper
3 tablespoons oil
¼ cup white vinegar

Buy liver in ½-inch slices. Dry slices on paper towels and place on a plate. Sprinkle with salt and allow to stand for at least 1 hour in refrigerator.
To cook, coat in flour mixed with pepper, and fry in heated oil in a frying pan for 5 minutes on either side or until tender. Lift onto a serving dish and keep warm. Drain off most of oil from pan, leaving 1 tablespoon. Add any seasoned flour left to the frying pan and mix into the oil. Cook a little, take pan off heat and pour in vinegar. Sauce will sizzle so take care. Return to heat and stir a little until bubbling and thick. Pour over liver and serve hot.
TIME 10 minutes.
GARNISH WITH chopped parsley.
SERVE WITH mashed potatoes and a green vegetable.
VARIATION use tarragon vinegar instead of white vinegar for a more piquant flavour.

BAKED LIVER AND ONIONS

Serves 4
1 large onion
¼ cup butter or margarine
½ cup red wine
½ cup water
¼ cup chopped parsley
1 bay leaf, crumbled
1 teaspoon dried thyme
1 teaspoon salt
freshly ground black pepper
4 slices beef liver
flour to coat

Slice onion thickly, place in base of an ovenproof dish and dot with butter. Pour in wine and water, add parsley, bay leaf, thyme, salt and pepper. Cover and cook in a moderate oven for 30 minutes. Coat liver with flour and place on top of onion slices. Cover and bake for 30 minutes, baste with liquid occasionally. Remove cover and bake for a further 10 minutes. Serve hot.
TIME 1¼ hours.
TEMPERATURE 350-375°F.
GARNISH WITH chopped parsley.
SERVE WITH baked jacket potatoes and a green vegetable.

CHOPPED LIVER AND EGG

Serves 4-6
½ lb lamb or veal liver
1 small onion
¼ cup butter or chicken fat
2 tablespoons soft breadcrumbs
2 tablespoons chopped parsley
1 hard-boiled egg
pinch of nutmeg
salt
freshly ground black pepper

Soak liver in cold water for 30 minutes. Remove skin if necessary and chop finely. Chop half the onion finely, put remainder aside until later. Sauté onion in 1 oz. butter or chicken fat until soft, add chopped liver and continue to cook until tender. Increase heat if juices run out so that liver is really fried, (takes about 4 minutes). Put cooked liver and onion through a food chopper using a fine blade, plus the remaining raw onion, breadcrumbs, parsley and egg. Mix in nutmeg, salt and pepper to taste, and enough soft butter or chicken fat (about 1 oz) to make a paste of a good spreading consistency. Shape Chopped Liver and Egg on 4-6 small individual plates and serve as an hors d'oeuvre.
TIME 8-10 minutes.
GARNISH WITH parsley sprigs.
SERVE WITH fingers of toast as a first course (hors d'oeuvre).
NOTE this is a popular Jewish dish.

LIVER PÂTÉ

Serves 6-8
1 lb lamb or veal liver
1 lb ground pork or pork and veal
1 clove garlic (½ if large), (optional)
3 green onions
1½ cups soft, fine breadcrumbs
2 eggs, lightly beaten
¼ cup dry sherry
2 tablespoons brandy
½ teaspoon dried marjoram
½ teaspoon dried thyme
½ teaspoon ground allspice
1½ teaspoons salt
freshly ground black pepper
bacon slices, rind removed

Put liver through food chopper, using finest blade. Put through chopper again with ground pork or pork and veal, garlic, if used, and green onions. Mix breadcrumbs with eggs and then mix into liver mixture with sherry, brandy, herbs, allspice and seasoning. Line a loaf tin with bacon slices and spoon in pâté mixture. Cover top with aluminium foil and bake in a moderately slow oven for 1¼-1½ hours, or until firm to the touch. Leave in tin to cool, pressing down with a light weight. Chill Liver Pâté in refrigerator.
To serve, unmould on to a platter and slice thinly.
TIME 1¼-1½ hours.
TEMPERATURE 325-350°F.
GARNISH WITH parsley sprigs.
SERVE WITH melba toast (thin slices of bread baked in a slow oven, 300-325°F. until crisp and golden), fingers of toast or wholemeal bread and butter if desired.

TRIPE AND ONIONS

Serves 4
1 lb tripe
cold water
2 white onions
2 teaspoons salt
3 tablespoons butter or margarine
3 tablespoons flour
1 cup liquid from tripe
1 cup milk
1 tablespoon chopped parsley
pepper if desired

Wash tripe, scrape underside if necessary, Blanch by placing in a saucepan of cold water, bring to the boil and pour off the water.
Cut blanched tripe into pieces 1-inch square. Replace in clean saucepan, cover with cold water, add peeled white onions and salt. Bring to the boil, reduce heat and simmer gently until tender (1½-3 hours: the time depends on the degree of cooking already done by the tripe preparers). Drain off liquid and reserve 1 cup. Place tripe on a plate, cut onion into pieces. In same saucepan (cleaned) melt butter and stir in flour. Cook over a medium heat for 1-2 minutes then pour in tripe liquid and milk and bring to the boil, stirring continuously, until thick and bubbling. Stir in tripe, onions, parsley and pepper if desired. Serve hot.
TIME 1½-3 hours.
GARNISH WITH chopped parsley and paprika.
SERVE WITH bacon rolls, toast triangles and a green vegetable.

CREAMED SWEETBREADS

Serves 4
1½ lb sweetbreads
juice of ½ lemon
2 tablespoons butter or margarine
salt
freshly ground black pepper
2 tablespoons semi-sweet sherry
1 cup Béchamel Sauce (see page 74)
¼ lb button mushrooms, sliced and sautéed in butter and lemon juice

Soak sweetbreads in cold water for 1 hour. Drain, place in a saucepan with cold water to cover, add lemon juice. Bring to simmering point and simmer gently for 15 minutes to blanch the sweetbreads—do not boil. When blanched, plunge sweetbreads into cold water to cool, then lift out and pull off skin and any fat or tubes. Cut sweetbreads diagonally in ½-inch slices and sauté in butter until lightly browned on all sides. Season with salt and pepper and add sherry. Cover and simmer gently for 5 minutes. Stir in Béchamel Sauce and sautéed mushrooms and cook until heated through. Serve hot with toast triangles.
TIME 30 minutes.
GARNISH WITH triangles of toast and a sprig of parsley.
SERVE WITH extra sautéed mushrooms if desired.
NOTE this dish is often served as a light entrée, rather than a main course.

SAUTÉED SWEETBREADS

Serves 4
1½ lb sweetbreads
¼ cup butter or margarine
salt and pepper
2 teaspoons lemon juice
2 teaspoons chopped parsley

Prepare and slice sweetbreads as for Creamed Sweetbreads. Melt butter in a frying pan and when sizzling, place sliced sweetbreads in pan and fry until browned on all sides. Place on a warm serving dish and season lightly with salt and pepper. To frying pan add the lemon juice and chopped parsley. Mix to blend in juices, taste and adjust flavor and pour over sweetbreads. Serve hot.
TIME 8 minutes.
GARNISH WITH sprig of parsley and lemon wedges.
SERVE WITH toast if desired.
NOTE this dish is often served as an entrée.

LAMBS' TONGUES WITH RAISIN SAUCE

Serves 4-6
6 lamb's tongues
1 onion
1 clove garlic
1 bay leaf
1 teaspoon salt

Raisin Sauce:
1 cup stock from tongues
⅓ cup raisins
¼ cup brown sugar
¼ cup dry white wine
1 tablespoon cornstarch
salt
freshly ground black pepper

Rinse tongues, place in saucepan and cover with cold water. Add peeled onion, garlic, bay leaf and salt. Bring to a slow boil, cover, reduce heat and simmer gently for at least 2 hours or until tongues are tender. Remove tongues, skin them and remove any bone and gristle from roots. Strain stock and reserve. To make Raisin Sauce return 1 cup stock to a clean saucepan, add raisins and brown sugar. Bring to the boil and stir in wine mixed with cornstarch to a smooth paste. Add salt and pepper to taste. Reduce heat and stir constantly until sauce thickens. Add tongues and simmer for 20 minutes. Serve tongues either whole or sliced lengthways in Raisin Sauce.
TIME 2½-3 hours.
GARNISH WITH parsley sprigs.
SERVE WITH mashed, sautéed or duchasse potatoes and a green vegetable.

SAUCES

STUFFINGS ETCETERA

71

PAN GRAVY
MUSHROOM SAUCE
WHITE SAUCE
OYSTER SAUCE
SWEET AND SOUR SAUCE
APRICOT BARBECUE SAUCE
SPICY TOMATO BARBECUE
  SAUCE
APPLE SAUCE
ONION SAUCE
TANGY MUSTARD SAUCE
BÉCHAMEL SAUCE
BÉARNAISE SAUCE   A
CURRIED CARROT SAUCE
CUMBERLAND SAUCE
SAGE AND ONION STUFFING
BASIC BISCUIT DOUGH
HERB AND BACON STUFFING B
PARSLEY DUMPLINGS

PLAIN PASTRY
YORKSHIRE PUDDING
HOT WATER CRUST PASTRY
FLAKY PASTRY
MUSHROOM STUFFING
PARSLEY BUTTER
MINT SAUCE
HORSERADISH SAUCE
ESPAGNOLE SAUCE
MADEIRA SAUCE
PIQUANT SAUCE

PAN GRAVY

Thin Gravy

Pour off all the fat from the roasting pan and reserve the pan juices and sediment. Add 1 cup meat stock or vegetable stock or 1 cup water and a bouillon cube. Place roasting pan over a high heat and bring to the boil, stirring continuously to dissolve and incorporate sediment. Add salt and pepper to taste.
Strain and serve gravy in a sauceboat.
SERVE WITH Roast Beef.

Thick Gravy

Pour off the fat from the roasting pan, reserving 2 tablespoons with the pan juices and sediment. Place roasting pan over a medium heat and sprinkle in 2 tablespoons all-purpose flour. Stir continuously with a wooden spoon until the mixture is smooth and begins to brown. Add 1 cup meat or vegetable stock or 1 cup water and a bouillon cube. Bring to the boil, stirring continuously. Add salt and pepper to taste.
Strain and serve gravy in a sauceboat.
SERVE WITH Roast Veal, Roast Lamb and Roast Pork.

MUSHROOM SAUCE

2 tablespoons chopped green onions
2 tablespoons butter or margarine
$\frac{1}{4}$ lb small mushrooms, sliced
1 teaspoon lemon juice
2 tablespoons all-purpose flour
$\frac{1}{4}$ cup dry white wine
1 cup light cream
salt
freshly ground black pepper

Sauté green onions in melted butter in a saucepan over a medium heat for 1 minute. Add mushrooms and lemon juice and sauté until mushrooms are cooked and liquid has evaporated. Add flour and cook, stirring, for 1-2 minutes. Add wine and $\frac{3}{4}$ cup cream, and bring to the boil, stirring constantly until sauce is thick and bubbling. Remove from heat and stir in remaining cream. Add seasoning to taste, if sauce is too thick add a little more wine.
SERVE WITH Roast Tenderloin of beef, broiled or pan-fried beef, veal or lamb.

WHITE SAUCE

2 tablespoons butter or margarine
2 tablespoons (1 cup) all-purpose flour
1 cup milk
$\frac{1}{2}$ teaspoon salt
white pepper

Melt butter or margarine in a saucepan over a low heat, stir in flour with a wooden spoon and cook gently for 1-2 minutes without coloring. Remove from heat, let bubbles subside and pour in milk at once, stirring continuously. Return to a moderate heat and bring to the boil, stirring continuously, until sauce thickens and bubbles. If the sauce becomes lumpy or you can see halfway through cooking that it might happen, use a wire balloon whisk to stir sauce and the lumps will disappear. In fact a balloon whisk may be used from the time the milk is poured in.
Season sauce to taste with salt and pepper. If a slightly thinner sauce is desired, add a little more milk and bring to the boil again. If sauce is to be kept for a while before using, place a piece of buttered greaseproof paper over surface of sauce and no skin will form. Reheat, stirring continuously before serving.
VARIATION add 2 tablespoons finely chopped parsley for Parsley Sauce. Add 2 oz grated cheddar cheese and a pinch of cayenne pepper, and stir over heat until cheese melts, for Cheese Sauce.
NOTE this sauce has a coating consistency and may be used for coating vegetables and is used in many recipes.

OYSTER SAUCE

$\frac{1}{4}$ pint oysters
2 tablespoons butter or margarine
1 tablespoon all-purpose flour
dry white wine
salt
freshly ground black pepper

Drain liquor from oysters and reserve. Cut each oyster in half if large. Melt butter in a saucepan over a low heat, stir in flour until well blended, without coloring. Add oyster liquor and bring to the boil, stirring continuously. Add enough white wine to give a good coating sauce consistency. Season with salt and pepper to taste.
SERVE WITH Carpet Bag Steak and broiled or pan-fried steak.

SWEET AND SOUR SAUCE

1½ cups cold water
½ cup carrots, cut in julienne strips
½ cup fresh pineapple, chopped
½ cup sugar
4 tablespoons vinegar
3 tablespoons soy sauce
1 tablespoon oil
½ cup sweet red or green pepper, cut in julienne strips
½ cup finely chopped green onions
3 thin slices fresh ginger root, chopped or ¼ teaspoon ground ginger
1 tablespoon cornstarch
salt and pepper

Bring 1½ cups cold water to the boil in a saucepan and cook carrot strips until just tender. Add pineapple pieces and cook for 1 minute. Stir in sugar, vinegar and soy sauce. Cover and simmer for 2 minutes.
Heat oil in a separate pan, and gently fry pepper strips for 1 minute. Add green onions, chopped ginger or powdered ginger and fry for a further 2 minutes. Add fried mixture to carrot mixture in saucepan. Blend cornstarch to a smooth paste with a little cold water and stir into mixture Bring to the boil, stirring continuously, until sauce thickens. Simmer for 2 minutes. Season to taste with salt and pepper and serve hot.
SERVE WITH Sweet and Sour Pork and Chinese Fried Pork Balls.

APRICOT BARBECUE SAUCE

3 tablespoons salad oil
2 tablespoons vinegar
½ cup apricot juice
½ cup tomato catsup
1 tablespoon brown sugar
2 tablespoons grated onion
½ teaspoon worcestershire sauce
1 teaspoon salt
½ teaspoon dried oregano
dash of tabasco sauce

Combine all ingredients together in a saucepan and bring to the boil, stirring occasionally. Cover and simmer gently for 10 minutes. Baste meat with Apricot Barbecue Sauce during barbecuing and serve remainder of sauce separately. This sauce keeps well for 1-2 weeks, if stored in a sealed container in a refrigerator.
SERVE WITH barbecued beef, lamb or pork.

SPICY TOMATO BARBECUE SAUCE

1 cup tomato catsup
2 tablespoons vinegar
1 tablespoon worcestershire sauce
1 tablespoon grated onion
2 tablespoons oil or butter
1 teaspoon sugar
1 teaspoon salt
½ teaspoon garlic powder
1 teaspoon paprika
½ teaspoon allspice
½ teaspoon dry mustard

Place all ingredients together in a saucepan and blend well until smooth. Bring to the boil over a low heat and simmer gently for 10 minutes. Baste meat with Spicy Tomato Barbecue Sauce during barbecuing and serve remainder of sauce separately. This sauce keeps for 1-2 weeks if stored in a sealed container in a refrigerator.
SERVE WITH barbecued beef, veal, lamb, kebabs and sausages.

APPLE SAUCE

3 green cooking apples
¼ cup water
1 teaspoon butter or margarine
sugar to taste
lemon juice to taste

Peel and core apples, slice into a saucepan and add water. Cover and simmer gently until soft enough to mash to a smooth pulp. If Apple Sauce contains too much liquid, reduce until the right consistency is obtained. Stir butter into warm sauce. Add sugar and lemon juice.
SERVE WITH Roast Pork, broiled or pan-fried pork chops.

ONION SAUCE

2 tablespoons butter or margarine
1 onion, sliced
2 tablespoons all-purpose flour
1 cup milk
salt and pepper

Melt butter in a saucepan over a low heat and sauté onion for 10 minutes, taking care not to brown it. Stir in flour and cook gently for 1-2 minutes, stirring continuously with a wooden spoon. Remove from heat, allow bubbles to subside and pour in milk, stirring continuously. Return to a moderate heat and bring to the boil stirring continuously until sauce thickens and bubbles. Simmer for 1 minute. Season to taste with salt and pepper before serving.
SERVE WITH Boiled Lamb, or Boiled Brisket.

TANGY MUSTARD SAUCE

2 tablespoons butter or margarine
2 tablespoons plain flour
1½ tablespoons dry mustard
1 tablespoon brown sugar
1½ teaspoons salt
1 cup milk
1 egg
3 tablespoons vinegar

Melt butter or margarine in a saucepan over low heat. Stir in flour, mustard, brown sugar and salt. Cook, stirring constantly, until well blended and bubbling. Add milk slowly, stirring continuously, and bring to the boil. Reduce heat and simmer sauce for 1 minute.
Beat egg slightly in a mixing bowl and gradually stir in half the hot sauce. Return egg mixture immediately to saucepan and cook for a further 1 minute over a low heat, stirring continuously. Remove sauce from heat, add vinegar and stir until evenly combined. Serve Tangy Mustard Sauce hot or cold.
SERVE WITH Corned Beef.

BECHAMEL SAUCE

1 cup milk
1 green onion, chopped
1 small carrot, sliced
1 small stalk celery, sliced
1 clove garlic
6 peppercorns
1 bay leaf
2 parsley stalks
2 tablespoons butter
2 tablespoons all-purpose flour
salt and pepper

Place milk in a saucepan with prepared vegetables, garlic, peppercorns, bay leaf and parsley stalks. Bring slowly to the boil. Remove from heat, cover and leave to infuse with flavorings for 30 minutes. Strain, discard flavoring ingredients and
½ cup dry white wine
Melt butter in a saucepan, stir in flour and cook over a low heat for 1-2 minutes, stirring continuously. Add warm milk gradually and bring to the boil, stirring continuously until sauce is thick and bubbling. Season with salt and pepper to taste. If desired, 2 tablespoons light cream may be stirred in for extra richness.
SERVE WITH veal dishes, in particular as the basic sauce for Veal Fricassée.

BÉARNAISE SAUCE

½ cup dry white wine
3 egg yolks
¼ cup tarragon vinegar
1 tablespoon finely chopped parsley
1 tablespoon finely chopped green onions
½ teaspoon dried tarragon or 1 table-spoon fresh, chopped tarragon
1 teaspoon dried chervil or 1 tablespoon fresh, chopped chervil
½ lb butter
½ teaspoon salt
freshly ground black pepper

Beat 1 tablespoon dry white wine into egg yolks and set aside. Combine the remaining wine with tarragon vinegar, parsley, shallots, tarragon and chervil in the top of a double boiler. Cook over direct heat until mixture reduces by one third in volume. Place water in bottom of double boiler and bring to simmering point. Place top of double boiler over bottom part and stir egg yolks mixed with wine into reduced mixture, stirring briskly with a whisk. Add butter, 2 oz at a time, stirring until each lot melts and blends into the sauce. When sauce is thick remove from heat, season with salt and pepper and strain into a sauceboat.
SERVE WITH Roast Tenderloin of Beef or broiled or pan-fried steak or lamb.

CURRIED CARROT SAUCE

1 cup carrots
1 large onion, chopped
2 tablespoons butter
1-2 teaspoons curry powder
2 tablespoons all-purpose flour
½ cup carrot liquor
½ cup milk
1 teaspoon tomato paste
½ teaspoon salt

Boil prepared carrots until tender, in just enough salted water to cover. Drain, reserve liquor and make up to ½ cup if necessary.
Sauté onion in melted butter in a saucepan, over a low heat, until soft. Stir in curry powder. Cook gently for 4 minutes, stirring continuously. Add flour and stir until well blended. Add carrot liquor and milk and bring to the boil, stirring constantly, until sauce thickens. Add cooked carrots, tomato paste and salt. Heat sauce through gently, simmer for 5 minutes and serve hot.
SERVE WITH Fruity Curried Meat Fingers (see page 28) and Beef Cobbler (see page 25).

CUMBERLAND SAUCE

2 tablespoons finely shredded orange rind
1 tablespoon finely shredded lemon rind
½ cup red currant jelly
½ cup fresh orange juice
2 tablespoons port wine
1 teaspoon dry mustard
1 tablespoon cornstarch
2 tablespoons lemon juice

Mix together orange and lemon rinds, (take care no pith remains when shredding) red currant jelly, orange juice, red wine and mustard. Heat until jelly melts and blends. Mix cornstarch into lemon juice and stir into heating orange mixture. Stir constantly until sauce boils and thickens. Allow to boil gently for 1 minute.
SERVE hot with baked ham or cold with Crust-Baked Smoked Picnic. (See page 89).

SAGE AND ONION STUFFING

2 tablespoons butter or fat
1 large onion, finely chopped
1½ cups soft breadcrumbs
2 teaspoons dried sage
½ teaspoon salt
freshly ground black pepper
beaten egg or water to bind

Melt butter in a saucepan over a low heat and sauté onion until soft. Mix into breadcrumbs with sage, seasoning and enough beaten egg or water to bind stuffing together. Use as required for stuffing a Crown Roast of Lamb (see page 43), boned legs or shoulders of meats, or for stuffing beef, calves' or lambs' hearts.

BASIC SCONE DOUGH

2 cups (8 oz) all-purpose flour
and 3 teaspoons baking powder
or 2 cups (8 oz) self-rising flour
½ teaspoon salt
¼ cup butter or margarine
¾ cup milk

Sift flour and baking powder or self-rising flour with salt into a mixing bowl. Rub butter into flour lightly with the fingertips until the mixture resembles fine breadcrumbs. Make a well in the center of the flour, pour in milk and mix with a round bladed knife to a soft dough. Turn on to a lightly floured board and knead very lightly until smooth (about 10 kneads). Roll out ½-inch thick and use as required.

HERB AND BACON STUFFING

2 slices bacon
1 small onion, finely chopped or grated
2 tablespoons butter or margarine
1½ cups soft breadcrumbs
2 tablespoons chopped parsley
½ teaspoon dried marjoram
½ teaspoon dried thyme
¼ teaspoon dried sage (optional)
½ teaspoon salt
freshly ground black pepper
beaten egg to bind

Remove rind from bacon and cut bacon into small pieces. Place bacon in a heated frying pan over a low heat and fry until almost crisp. Add onion and butter and continue to fry gently until onion is soft. Mix into breadcrumbs with herbs, salt and pepper. Add sufficient beaten egg to bind stuffing together and use as required to stuff various joints of meat for roasting or pot roasting.
NOTE this stuffing may be used for Beef Olives and Veal Birds. Substitute bacon with the grated rind and juice of 1 lemon for a more delicate flavour.

PARSLEY DUMPLINGS

1 cup all-purpose flour
2 teaspoons baking powder
½ teaspoon salt
2 tablespoons butter or margarine
1 egg
2 tablespoons finely chopped parsley
½ cup milk

Sift flour, baking powder and salt into a mixing bowl. Rub butter in lightly with the fingertips. Beat egg and mix with parsley and milk. Add egg mixture to flour and mix to a soft dough. Scoop out dough with a wet tablespoon and drop quickly on top of a bubbling stew. Keep the dumplings away from the sides of the pan or casserole to allow a little space for heat to circulate. Cover and cook gently for 15 minutes. Serve dumplings with stew.

PLAIN PASTRY

2 cups all-purpose flour
½ teaspoon salt
½ cup lard or margarine
3-4 tablespoons cold water

Sift flour and salt into a mixing bowl. Mix shortening into the flour, using 2 knives or a pastry blender, until the mixture resembles fine breadcrumbs. Add cold water gradually and mix with a round bladed knife to a stiff dough which should leave the sides of the bowl cleanly. Knead pastry lightly until smooth. Wrap pastry and chill. Roll out and use as required.

YORKSHIRE PUDDING

Serves 4-6
1 cup (4 oz) all-purpose flour
pinch of salt
1 egg
1 cup milk

Sift flour and salt together into a mixing bowl. Make a well in the center and drop in the whole egg. Add half the milk, a little at a time, and gradually stir in the flour from the sides of the bowl using a wooden spoon. Mix until smooth then beat batter with the back of the spoon for 5-10 minutes. When thoroughly beaten air bubbles appear on the surface. Cover and allow batter to stand for 30 minutes. Stir in remaining milk, to give a thin batter, just before cooking. Grease muffin pans or a shallow square 9-inch cake tin with drippings from roast beef and place in a very hot oven until fat is smoking hot. Remove muffin pans and quickly pour in batter to come halfway up each pan. Return to a very hot oven and cook until Yorkshire Pudding is crisp, puffed up and golden brown. Serve at once.
TIME 15-20 minutes for individual Yorkshire Puddings. 30-40 minutes for a large Yorkshire Pudding.
TEMPERATURE 450-500°F.
SERVE WITH Roast Beef (see page 20).

HOT WATER CRUST PASTRY

3 cups (12 oz) all-purpose flour
1 teaspoon salt
1 cup milk and water, mixed
4½ oz (1 cup plus 1 tablespoon) lard

Sift flour and salt into a mixing bowl and place in a warm oven to warm the flour. Place milk and water with the lard into a small saucepan and bring to the boil slowly. Pour mixture, whilst bubbling, into the warmed flour and mix with a wooden spoon until the dough leaves the sides of the bowl clean. Work and shape pastry quickly, rolling first piece out on a floured board while remainder is kept warm in bowl covered with a cloth. If pastry is allowed to cool too much it cracks and is difficult to handle.
NOTE This is the traditional pastry used in England for raised pork, veal and ham, game pies etc., which are usually served cold.

FLAKY PASTRY

3 cups (12 oz) all-purpose flour
pinch of salt
9 oz firm butter or margarine
½ teaspoon lemon juice
cold water to mix

Sift flour and salt together into a mixing bowl. Divide shortening into four equal portions. Rub one portion into the flour with the fingertips. Using a round bladed knife, mix with lemon juice and cold water to a pliable soft dough. Roll out dough to an oblong, about 12 x 5-inches, keeping edges straight and corners square. Brush off excess flour with a pastry brush. Mark oblong into thirds lightly with a knife. Place a portion of shortening on top ⅔ of dough in little pieces. Sprinkle lightly with flour and fold bottom ⅓ of pastry up over middle ⅓ and fold top ⅓ down. Press edges lightly together with a rolling pin. Turn dough a ¼ turn so folded edges are to right and left. Roll out and fold as before including another portion of the shortening. Cover dough with clear plastic and chill for 30 minutes. Roll, fold and include final portion of shortening as before. Cover dough and chill again for 30 minutes. Roll and fold once more. Use as required.
NOTE equal quantities of butter and lard may be used instead of all butter. Mix both fats together thoroughly before dividing into four portions. A point to remember is that when a recipe stipulates the use of 12 oz Flaky Pastry, for example, this means to use a quantity of pastry taking 12 oz flour.

MUSHROOM STUFFING

2 tablespoons butter or margarine
1 small onion, chopped or ¼ cup chopped green onions
¼ lb mushrooms, chopped
2 teaspoons lemon juice
1½ cups soft breadcrumbs
2 tablespoons chopped parsley
½ teaspoon salt
freshly ground black pepper

Melt butter or margarine in a saucepan over a low heat and sauté onion or shallots until just soft. Add mushrooms and lemon juice and cook until mushrooms are tender. Mix into breadcrumbs, with parsley, salt and pepper. Use as required to stuff Beef Olives or Veal Birds (see page 25, 48) as an alternative to given recipe. Also good for stuffing joints of meat for roasting.

PARSLEY BUTTER
Mâitre d'hôtel butter

¼ lb butter
2 tablespoons lemon juice
2 tablespoons finely chopped parsley
½ teaspoon salt
freshly ground black pepper

Cream butter with a wooden spoon until soft. Beat in lemon juice, chopped parsley, salt and pepper. When evenly blended turn butter mixture onto a piece of waxed paper or clear plastic and shape into a cylinder or a long, thin rectangle. Wrap and chill in a refrigerator until required. Cut into ½-inch slices to serve. Wrap remaining Parsley Butter and store in refrigerator.
SERVE WITH Broiled Steak; Veal or Lamb.
VARIATION to make Garlic Butter, substitute lemon juice with 2 cloves of crushed garlic.
To make Anchovy Butter, substitute 8-10 pounded or sieved anchovy fillets for chopped parsley and omit the salt.
NOTE Table margarine may be used instead of butter.

MINT SAUCE

¼ cup fresh, chopped mint
2 tablespoons sugar
2 tablespoons boiling water
¼ cup vinegar

Place chopped mint in a small sauceboat. Add sugar and boiling water. Stir until sugar is dissolved. Add vinegar, stir and leave to stand at least 15 minutes before serving.
SERVE WITH Roast Lamb.

HORSERADISH SAUCE

1 cup Béchamel Sauce
2 teaspoons cream
2 teaspoons sugar
3 tablespoons prepared horseradish
salt
white pepper

Make Béchamel Sauce according to given recipe (see page 74). Add cream, sugar, horseradish and stir in until evenly blended. Add salt and pepper to taste. Serve Horseradish Sauce hot or cold.
SERVE WITH Roast Beef and Beef Tongue.

ESPAGNOLE SAUCE

1 slice bacon
¼ cup butter or fat
1 onion
1 carrot
⅓ cup flour
2 cups stock (see page 80)
bouquet garni
pinch of salt
freshly ground black pepper
½ cup chopped tomato
6 small mushrooms
¼ cup sherry

Cut bacon into small pieces and fry in melted butter in a heavy based saucepan. Cut onion and carrot into chunky pieces, add to pan and fry slowly over a low heat until golden brown, about 10-15 minutes. Stir in flour and continue cooking gently for 10 minutes until flour is golden brown. Add stock, bouquet garni, salt and pepper and bring to the boil. Stir to loosen any sediment. Cover and simmer gently for 1 hour. Add tomato and chopped mushrooms when half cooked.
Strain sauce through a pointed strainer. Do not sieve. Return to a clean saucepan. Add sherry, reheat and adjust flavor and consistency if necessary before serving.
SERVE WITH Bacon-Wrapped Filet Mignon, T-Bone Steak, Tournedos or Roast Tenderloin of Beef.

MADEIRA SAUCE

1 cup Espagnole Sauce
¼ cup Madeira wine
½ teaspoon meat or vegetable extract

Heat the Espagnole Sauce in a saucepan. Add Madeira wine and meat extract and reheat. Reduce by simmering without lid to adjust consistency if necessary.
SERVE WITH hot Baked, Glazed Corned Brisket.

PIQUANT SAUCE

2 green onions, finely chopped
1 bay leaf
1 teaspoon dried thyme
½ cup vinegar
1 cup Espagnole Sauce
2 gherkins, chopped
1 tablespoons chopped capers
salt
cayenne pepper

Place the green onions, bay leaf, thyme and vinegar into a saucepan and boil until reduced to half the quantity. Add Espagnole Sauce and simmer for 20 minutes. Strain through a pointed strainer. Add gherkins, capers and salt and cayenne pepper to taste. Reheat before serving.
SERVE WITH Lambs' Tongues, Lamb's Liver or Pan-Fried Lamb Steaks.

SOUPS

BEEF AND VEGETABLE SOUP

Serves 6
3 pints Beef Bone Stock (with fat removed)
2-3 tablespoons fat from stock
1 large onion, chopped
1 cup diced carrots
½ cup diced celery
½ cup diced turnip
¼ cup diced parsnip
1½ lb shank cross cuts
1 cup chopped tomatoes
1 teaspoon sugar
1 tablespoon salt
½ teaspoon pepper

Prepare stock according to recipe and reserve required fat. Place fat in soup kettle or large saucepan and sauté onions, carrots, celery, turnip and parsnip over a low heat for 10 minutes. Increase heat and add boned and diced shanks. Cook, stirring, until beef juices run out and brown. Add stock, tomatoes, sugar, salt and pepper. Bring to boil, reduce heat, cover and simmer for 1¼ hours or until beef is tender. Serve immediately or keep for a day before serving as flavor improves on keeping. If desired, add ¼ cup pearl barley when stock is added, in which case do not keep soup too long before serving as the starch in the soup will cause deterioration more rapidly. Always store soup under refrigeration.
TIME 1¼-1½ hours.
GARNISH WITH finely chopped parsley.
SERVE WITH croûtons.
NOTE the browning of the meat juices before adding liquid eliminates the need to skim soup, and makes the soup richer.

BEEF TEA

Serves 2
½ lb round or boneless sirloin steak
1 cup cold water
pinch of salt
few drops lemon juice

Wipe beef with a damp cloth and remove all fat. Shred or mince beef very finely. Place in a mixing bowl with water, salt and lemon juice, cover and allow to stand for 1 hour.
Place beef mixture in the top of a double boiler (water in bottom part must be just simmering) and stir over a low heat until meat changes color and becomes hot. Press meat during cooking to extract juices. Strain Beef Tea into a bowl and serve hot with toast.
TIME 5-10 minutes.
GARNISH WITH sprig of parsley.
SERVE WITH sippets of toast.
NOTE this is of great benefit to invalids and the convalescing as the slow, low heat method of cooking retains all the goodness of the beef in an easily digestible form. If the Beef Tea boils, the albumen, which is the protein or flesh forming element of the juice of the meat, will harden above 150°F. It mixes freely with cold water, and remains soluble as long as the heat is not too great. Once the albumen is allowed to coagulate, it either hardens the meat itself or forms a coarse sediment which will not pass through the strainer, thus losing one of the most valuable properties of Beef Tea. This recipe is quicker to preapre than most, but the nutritive value does not suffer.

BEEF BONE STOCK

Yield: 3 pints
4 lb meaty soup bones sawn in pieces
1 onion, halved
2 carrots, quartered
1 outer stalk celery, cut in 3 pieces
1 small turnip, sliced
12 peppercorns
1 bay leaf
4 parsley stalks
pinch of dried thyme
1 tablespoon salt

Wash bones in cold water, place in a large kettle and cover with cold water (about 4 pints). Bring slowly to the boil, skimming when necessary. Add vegetables, peppercorns, herbs and salt. Cover and simmer for 2-3 hours, skimming if necessary. Remove any fat and strain stock into a large bowl, discard bones and vegetables. Cover Beef Bone Stock and store in refrigerator.
TIME 3 hours.
USE FOR making soups, stews, casseroles and gravy.
NOTE An easier way to remove fat is to strain stock into a container, place it in the refrigerator and chill until fat sets on top. Lift off and discard.

BORSCH

Serves 6
2½ lb beef shank cross cuts
1 lb beef brisket, cut in 1-inch pieces
2 large onions, chopped
3 cups canned tomatoes
3 cups shredded cabbage
2 cups diced pared beets
½ cup lemon juice
4 cloves garlic, crushed
¼ cup chopped parsley
1 small bay leaf
1 teaspoon paprika
2 tablespoons sugar
2 teaspoons salt
freshly ground black pepper
sour cream

Rinse meats in cold water. Place in a kettle or large saucepan and cover with cold water. Bring to the boil, skimming when necessary, reduce heat, cover and boil gently for 1 hour. Add onions, tomatoes, cabbage, beets, lemon juice, garlic, herbs, paprika, sugar and seasoning Simmer for 2 hours. Remove any bones and discard, lift out meat and cut into 1-inch pieces. Skim off as much fat as possible from soup surface. Return meat to soup and simmer for 10 minutes. Taste and adjust seasoning and serve Borsch with a bowl of sour cream for topping each plate of soup.
TIME 3 hours.
GARNISH WITH a soup spoon of sour cream on each serving.
SERVE WITH wholemeal or rye bread, thickly sliced and buttered to make a meal in itself.

CUCUMBER AND MEAT SLICE SOUP

Serves 6
½ lb flank skirt steak
3 lb beef soup bones, sawn into pieces
2 green cucumbers

Marinade:
1 tablespoon oil
2 tablespoons dry sherry
2-inch piece of fresh ginger root
½ teaspoon sugar
1 teaspoon salt
freshly ground black pepper

Slice flank steak into paper thin slices (it is easier to do this if the meat is partially frozen). Mix marinade ingredients together and add sliced steak. Allow to marinate for 1 hour.
Wash soup bones and place in a pot or large pan with the cucumber, sliced ¼-inch thick, and cover with 3 pints boiling water. Bring back to the boil, reduce heat and simmer, covered, for 45 minutes, skimming when necessary. Remove bones and add beef and marinade to the stock and simmer without boiling for 10 minutes. Skim off fat, taste and adjust seasoning and serve immediately.
TIME 55 minutes.
GARNISH WITH thin slices of par-boiled cucumber.
SERVE WITH soy sauce.

MULLIGATAWNY SOUP

Serves 4-6
3 lb lamb neck slices and fore shanks
2 tablespoons butter or margarine
2 onions, chopped
2 carrots, chopped
2 green apples, peeled and chopped
1 small turnip, chopped
2 tablespoons curry powder
3 tablespoons flour
1 bay leaf, 1 celery top,
3 parsley stalks, tied together
2 tablespoons lemon juice
salt

Ask meat retailer to saw shanks into pieces 2-inches thick. Rinse meat in cold water, place in kettle or large saucepan and cover with cold water. Bring to boil slowly, skimming when necessary. Cover and simmer over a low heat for 1 hour. Skim fat from surface. Melt butter in a pan and sauté onion, carrot, apple and turnip for 15 minutes. Stir in curry powder and cook, stirring for 5 minutes. Add flour and blend well. Leave aside, off heat, until stock is ready. Add vegetable-curry mixture to stock with flavoring herbs. Cover and simmer for 2½ hours or until meat is tender. Take out chunks of meat and trim off lean meat when cool enough to handle; chop finely. Sieve soup into another pan, discard flavoring bouquet, and press vegetables through sieve into soup. Add pieces of meat, reheat. Add lemon juice, taste and adjust seasoning.
TIME 2½ hours.
GARNISH WITH finely chopped parsley.
SERVE WITH a bowl of hot boiled rice.

SCOTCH BROTH

Serves 6
1½-2 lb lamb neck slices
3 pints water
¼ cup pearl barley
1 tablespoon salt
1 outer stalk celery, diced
1 large carrot, diced
1 onion, diced
1 turnip, diced
1 leek, diced
freshly ground black pepper
2 tablespoons chopped parsley

Remove as much fat as possible from meat and any loose bones. Cut meat into pieces, place in a deep saucepan and cover with the water. Bring slowly to the boil, skimming when necessary. Add washed barley and salt and simmer, covered, for 30 minutes. Add diced vegetables and cook for a further 1½-2 hours or until meat is tender.
Lift out meat pieces, trim off as much lean meat as possible and cut into small pieces. Return to broth and stir in pepper to taste, more salt if necessary and parsley.
TIME 2-2½ hours.
GARNISH WITH chopped parsley.
SERVE WITH crusty bread.

OXTAIL SOUP

Serves 4-6
2-3 lb oxtail (oxjoint) slices
2 tablespoons fat
2 onions, chopped
2 carrots, chopped
1 cup sliced celery
3 pints water
1 bay leaf and 4 parsley stalks tied together
½ teaspoon dried thyme or a sprig of fresh thyme
½ teaspoon dried marjoram or a sprig of fresh marjoram
bacon rinds (if available)
2 teaspoons salt
freshly ground black pepper
cornstarch
lemon juice to taste

Wash and blanch oxtail, drain and dry with paper towels. Melt fat in large saucepan and brown oxtail on all sides. Lift out and drain. Add vegetables to pan and fry until lightly browned. Add water, herbs, bacon rinds, seasoning and browned oxtails. Bring to a slow boil, skimming if necessary, reduce heat, cover and simmer for 3 hours or until meat is tender. Lift out meat and bacon rinds. Skim fat from soup. Remove meat from pieces of oxtail and shred. Return shredded meat to soup. Thicken soup with cornstarch blended to a smooth paste with a little cold water if desired. Taste soup and adjust seasoning, stir in lemon juice to taste and serve.
TIME 3-4 hours.
GARNISH WITH chopped parsley.
SERVE WITH crusty bread.

BARBECUE MEATS

PINEAPPLE BARBECUED LAMB SHANKS   C
MARINATED BARBECUE STEAKS OR CHOPS   A
BARBECUED SIRLOIN STEAK
SESAME FLAVORED STEAKS
TERIYAKI KEBABS
BARBECUED SAUSAGES   B
BARBECUED HAMBURGERS
SHISH KEBABS

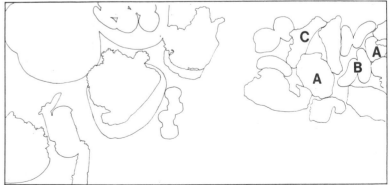

PINEAPPLE BARBECUED LAMB SHANKS

Serves 4
8 lamb foreshanks
1 x 1 lb or 1½ lb can pineapple slices

Marinade:
1 cup pineapple juice
2 teaspoons curry powder
3 tablespoons brown sugar
1 clove garlic, crushed
1 teaspoon salt
freshly ground black pepper
3 tablespoons salad oil

Wipe shanks with a damp cloth and place them in a single layer in a glass, earthenware or enamel dish. Mix marinade ingredients, adding to them the liquid drained from the pineapple slices. (Store slices in an air-tight plastic container in refrigerator until barbecue time). Pour marinade over shanks and marinate for at least 4 hours, turning them occasionally.
To barbecue, place shanks over glowing coals and cook for 25-30 minutes, turning often and basting with marinade. Place pineapple slices on barbecue 5 minutes before shanks are cooked.
TIME 25-30 minutes.
GARNISH WITH barbecued pineapple slices.
SERVE WITH salad and French bread and butter.

MARINATED BARBECUE STEAKS OR CHOPS

Serves 4
4 slices barbecue steak or barbecue lamb chops (see pages 18, 52 for suitable barbecue meats)

Soy Marinade:
½ cup soy sauce
1 clove garlic, finely chopped
freshly ground black pepper
monosodium glutamate (optional)

Place steaks or chops in a large mixing bowl. Mix marinade ingredients and pour over meat and marinate for at least 30 minutes. Lift meat out of marinade and drain a little. Place meat on barbecue over glowing coals and cook for 3-4 minutes on either side, or less if you prefer medium rare meat.
TIME 30 minutes to marinate, 8 minutes to cook.
GARNISH WITH salad vegetables.
SERVE WITH barbecue sauce, salad, buttered bread rolls or foil-baked jacket potatoes.

BARBECUED SIRLOIN STEAK

Serves 4-6
1 slice sirloin steak cut 2½-inches thick
freshly ground black pepper
salt
Apricot or Tomato Barbecue Sauce (see page 73), optional

Rub surface of steak with freshly ground black pepper. Place over glowing coals and sear quickly on either side to seal in the meat juices. Lift off barbecue onto a piece of heavy foil (using tongs) and fold over foil, sealing it well on all sides. Replace on barbecue and cook for 10 minutes on either side for medium rare steak, an extra 3 minutes on either side for medium steak. Take care not to pierce foil when turning.
To serve, lift steak out of foil onto a wooden platter and carve in a slanting position, into 1-inch wide slices. If desired, serve with one of the barbecue sauces mentioned above.
TIME 25-30 minutes.
GARNISH WITH lettuce and tomato.
SERVE WITH baked jacket potatoes and a tossed green salad.

SESAME FLAVOURED STEAKS

Serves 4
4 T-bone steaks, ¾-inch thick, (or sirloin, porterhouse or club)

Marinade:
2 tablespoons salad oil
1 teaspoon lemon juice
¼ cup soy sauce
1 tablespoon brown sugar
2 tablespoons grated onion or chopped green onions
freshly ground black pepper
¼ teaspoon garlic powder
¼ teaspoon ground ginger
pinch of monosodium glutamate
2 tablespoons sesame seeds

Place steak in a flat dish, cut in four portions if necessary. Combine marinade ingredients and pour over steaks. Marinate for 1 hour, turning steaks two or three times. To barbecue, lift meat out of marinade and place over glowing coals. Cook for 6-8 minutes on either side, according to taste and type of steak used. Cook longer for well done steak but barbecued steak is much better medium done. Brush with marinade during cooking.
TIME 1 hour to marinate, 12-16 minutes to cook.
GARNISH WITH salad greens.
SERVE WITH salads baked jacket potatoes and garlic bread.

TERIYAKI KEBABS

Serves 4
1 lb boneless sirloin steak cut 1-inch thick (top round steak may be used)
1 x 1 lb can pineapple chunks
stuffed olives

Marinade:
¼ cup soy sauce
1 tablespoon dry white wine or lemon juice
1 clove garlic, finely chopped
1 tablespoon oil

Trim excess fat from steak and cut into long strips 3-4-inches long and ¼-inch wide. For easier slicing partially freeze meat. Mix marinade ingredients in a mixing bowl, add steak strips and coat well with marinade. Leave to stand for ½ hour. Marinate round steak for 3 hours. To prepare kebabs, take out strips of steak and drain. Weave each strip onto a skewer, piercing an olive or a pineapple chunk onto skewer each time you pass it through the meat. To fill skewer a second piece of steak may be needed. This quantity should fill six skewers at least, depending on the length of skewers. Place over glowing coals and barbecue quickly, turning often, and brushing with marinade.
TIME 3-5 minutes.
GARNISH WITH pineapple and parsley sprigs.
SERVE WITH rice and tossed green salad.

BARBECUED SAUSAGES

Serves 4-6
2 lb pork sausages (raw)
Apricot Barbecue Sauce (see page 73)

Unwind sausages carefully and place them in a saucepan in links of 3-5 sausages. Cover with water and bring slowly to simmering point. Take off heat and leave in water to cool. Drain and dry when cooled and store in a sealed container in refrigerator until time to barbecue. This par-boiling gives sausages which will not ooze out or shrivel when exposed to the heat of the coals.
Barbecue sausages over glowing coals, turning often and basting with Apricot Barbecue Sauce. Cook sausages for 6-8 minutes. Serve with remaining barbecue sauce, reheated in pan on side of barbecue.
TIME 6-8 minutes.
GARNISH WITH salad vegetables.
SERVE WITH French bread and salad.

BARBECUED HAMBURGERS

Serves 6-8
1½ lb ground beef
1½ teaspoons salt
freshly ground black pepper
1 small grated onion
½ cup dry breadcrumbs
½ cup evaporated milk
¼ teaspoon monosodium glutamate
8 hamburger buns

Place hamburger steak into a mixing bowl with salt, pepper and grated onion. Soak breadcrumbs in evaporated milk and mix lightly into meat until well blended. Shape meat into eight thick patties, pack into a dish with plastic wrap between and on top of each layer. Refrigerate until time to take to barbecue. Cook over glowing coals for 4-6 minutes on either side. Baste whilst cooking with either Apricot or Spicy Tomato Barbecue Sauce (see page 73), if desired.
Toast split buns over coals, place hamburgers on buttered base, top with cooked pineapple slices, sliced tomatoes, onions and lettuce. If the hamburgers are not basted, add tomato sauce, mustard pickles or chutney on top of hamburger itself. Top with buttered bun and serve.
TIME 8-12 minutes.
GARNISH WITH sliced pineapple, tomatoes, onion rings and lettuce.
SERVE WITH buttered hamburger buns, barbecue sauce, tomato catsup, mustard pickles or chutney.

SHISH KEBABS

Serves 4-6
2 lb lamb steak cut 1-inch thick or, for economy, use boned lamb riblets
12 button onions or 6 medium onions
1 green pepper
1 sweet red pepper
3-4 bay leaves broken in large pieces (optional)
salt

Marinade:
3 tablespoons salad oil
3 tablespoons wine vinegar or lemon juice
2 cloves garlic, crushed
2 tablespoons grated onion or finely chopped green onion
1 crumbled bay leaf
freshly ground black pepper

Trim excess fat from lamb and cut into 1-inch cubes. Par-boil onions, cutting larger ones in half lengthways. Wash and remove stem and seeds from peppers and cut into 1-inch squares. Mix marinade ingredients in a bowl and add lamb pieces. Allow to marinate for 1 hour, turning meat occasionally. To prepare kebabs, thread onto 4-6 skewers alternatively, lamb pieces, onions, green and red peppers and bay leaves. Brush with marinade and barbecue over glowing coals for 4-6 minutes, turn and brush with marinade during cooking. Serve immediately.
TIME 4-6 minutes.
GARNISH WITH barbecued tomatoes.
SERVE WITH tossed green salad.
VARIATION try basting with Apricot or Spicy Tomato Barbecue Sauce (see page 73).

SALAD MEATS

OLIVE STUDDED BEEF   G
SPICED SHOULDER OF LAMB WITH ROSEMARY
RAISED PORK PIE   E
PICNIC MEAT LOAF   D
BOILED CORNED BRISKET   B
CRUST BAKED SMOKED PICNIC   A
MEAT ASPIC   F
PRESSED TONGUE   C

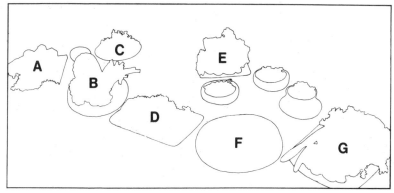

OLIVE STUDDED BEEF

Serves 6-8
1 x 3-4 lb sir'oin tip, cap on, or rolled rump
stuffed green olives
salt
freshly ground black pepper

Weigh meat to calculate cooking time. Cut slits, evenly spaced in rows, on top surface of meat. Make the cuts the length of the olives to be used and just deep enough to imbed an olive on its side into each slit. Tie sirloin tip with string at intervals to give it a more rounded shape if necessary. Rub salt on top and sprinkle top and meat surface with pepper. Place meat on a rack in a roasting pan and roast in a moderately slow oven for 30 minutes per lb for rare, plus a further 30 minutes for medium done beef. Insert a meat thermometer to check degree of cooking if desired. As this is a recipe for outdoor eating and is to be eaten cold, it is much better for meat to be at least medium done as well done beef is too dry when cold.
TIME 30 minutes per lb for rare beef plus 30 minutes extra for medium cooked beef.
TEMPERATURE 325-350°F.
GARNISH WITH stuffed olives and parsley.
SERVE WITH salad and mustard.
NOTE if you would like this served hot as a main meal, make gravy from pan drippings according to directions on page 72.

SPICED SHOULDER OF LAMB WITH ROSEMARY.

Serves 4-6
1 boned shoulder of lamb
1 tablespoon dried or fresh rosemary spikes, or 1 teaspoon ground rosemary
3 tablespoons brown sugar
2 tablespoons flour
1 teaspoon salt
½ teaspoon ground allspice
½ teaspoon ground ginger
pinch of nutmeg
¼ cup melted butter or margarine
2 tablespoons vinegar
2 tablespoons tomato catsup

Open out shoulder of lamb and make slits on both sides if using rosemary spikes. Insert spikes into slits. If using dried, ground rosemary just sprinkle over both surfaces. Combine remaining ingredients, in order given, and spread half mixture over inner surface. Roll up and tie into a neat roll with white string. Place lamb in a roasting pan, pour remaining mixture over shoulder and bake in a moderately slow oven, for 1½-2 hours, depending on quality of lamb used. Serve cold.
TIME 1½-2 hours.
TEMPERATURE 325-350°F.
GARNISH WITH watercress or parsley sprigs.
SERVE WITH mint sauce or jelly and mixed salad.
NOTE this dish can be served hot as a main course.

RAISED PORK PIE

Serves 4
1 lb lean pork
1 small apple, peeled and diced
pinch of allspice or ground cloves
1 teaspoon salt
freshly ground black pepper
2 teaspoons arrowroot
12 oz Hot Water Crusty Pastry (see page 76)
stock made from veal bones

Cut pork into 1-inch cubes. Mix with apple, allspice or cloves, salt, pepper and arrowroot. Line a greased raised pie mold with ⅔ Hot Water Crusty Pastry. Fill with pork mixture and mositen edges of pastry. Roll out remaining pastry to fit top and place over pie. Press sides together to seal, cut off excess pastry. Roll extra pastry out, cut and shape into decorations. Brush pie with beaten egg, place decorations on and brush with egg. Cut a vent in center of pie to allow steam to escape. A pastry rose may be put into this. Bake in a hot oven for 45 minutes, reduce heat to moderately slow and bake a further 1½-2 hours or until pork is tender (test with a skewer through vent). Remove mold, brush sides with beaten egg and replace in oven to brown Pour strained hot stock through vent, replace decoration and leave pie to cool until set. Serve cold.
TIME 2¾-3¼ hours.
TEMPERATURE 400-450°F reducing to 325-350°F.
GARNISH WITH parsley sprigs and tomato.
SERVE WITH mixed salad.

PICNIC MEAT LOAF

Serves 6-8
1½ lb finely minced beef
½ lb sausage mince
2 slices bacon, finely chopped
1 onion, finely chopped
½ green pepper, grated
1½ teaspoon salt
¼ teaspoon pepper
1 cup soft breadcrumbs
1 cup evaporated milk
3 hard-boiled eggs

Place steak and sausage mince into a mixing bowl. Fry bacon with onion in a frying pan for 10 minutes. Drain off fat and cool. Add fried bacon and onion to meats, with salt and pepper. Soak breadcrumbs in evaporated milk and mix into other ingredients lightly until well blended. Lift mixture onto a moistened board and flatten out a little down center. Place shelled hard-boiled eggs along center. Mould up each side of meat mixture over the eggs and press ends and top well together to seal. Lift carefully and place, joined side down, in a greased baking dish, pat into an even shaped roll and bake in a moderate oven for 1¼ hours. Baste with drippings from meat during cooking. When cooked, cool and wrap in plastic wrap or place in a sealed container, then store in refrigerator until picnic time.
TIME 1¼ hours.
TEMPERATURE 350-375°F.
GARNISH WITH lettuce, tomato or radishes and celery curls.
SERVE WITH salad.

BOILED, CORNED BRISKET

Serves 6-8
1 x 3-4 lb piece corned beef or brisket-rolled
1 tablespoon brown sugar
12 whole peppercorns
1 bay leaf
1 tablespoon vinegar

Weigh corned beef and calculate cooking time. Rinse in cold water, place in a deep saucepan and cover with cold water. Add brown sugar, peppercorns, bay leaf and vinegar. Bring to simmering point and simmer, covered, for required time. Cool in liquid. Remove and wrap closely. Store in refrigerator till needed.
TIME 30 minutes per lb plus 30 minutes extra.
GARNISH WITH lettuce or watercress and tomato.
SERVE WITH salad and pickles or chutney.

CRUST-BAKED SMOKED PICNIC

Serves 12
1 x 5 lb smoked Picnic Shoulder (cook before eating)
1 lb all-purpose flour
cold water to mix

Soak Picnic in cold water for at least 24 hours. Remove, drain and pat completely dry with cloth and paper towels. Place flour into a basin and mix in enough cold water to give a workable dough. Roll out on a floured board in a large rectangle. Place Picnic Shoulder in center and bring up sides of dough to cover ham. Moisten edges with water and seal well at all joins. Lift carefully into a large baking dish and bake in a moderate oven for 3 hours. Remove from oven, allow ham to cool in crust. When cool break off crust and discard. Place ham in a container, seal and refrigerate until required for your picnic.
TIME 3 hours (35 minutes per pound).
GARNISH WITH pineapple slices.
SERVE WITH assorted salads.

MEAT ASPIC

Serves 6-8
1 Veal foreshank, sawn in slices
1½ lb corned brisket (on the bone)
½ lb salt pork
3 whole allspice
6 peppercorns
1 bay leaf
3 sprigs parsley
1 stalk celery, cut in 3 pieces
1 large onion, sliced
1 large carrot, sliced
2 tablespoons unflavored gelatin
Vinegar to taste
salt
Rinse meats, place in kettle and just cover with water. Add remaining ingredients except gelatin, vinegar and salt. Bring to boil slowly, skimming when necessary Cover and simmer for 2½ hours or until meats are tender. Strain stock through muslin into a bowl and refrigerate to set fat for easy removal. Dice all lean pieces of meat and set aside. Discard fat, bones and flavoring ingredients. Remove fat from stock. Measure 3 cups into a clean pan, heat a little if it has "gelled". Dissolve gelatin in ¼ cup of stock over hot water, add to stock with meat. Add vinegar and salt to taste. Pour into a mold (first rinsed in water) and refrigerate until set.
TIME 2½-3 hours.
GARNISH WITH Tomato wedges.
SERVE WITH potato salad and a tossed green salad.

PRESSED TONGUE

Serves 8
1 pickled or corned beef tongue
1 onion
2 carrots
1 stalk celery
1 bay leaf
3 cloves
6 peppercorns

Scrub tongue under running water. Soak in cold water for at least 24 hours. Place in a deep pan, cover with fresh, cold water and add onion, carrots, top of stalk celery, bay leaf, cloves and peppercorns. Bring to a slow boil, reduce heat, cover and simmer for 3 hours or until tender (test with a skewer, which should penetrate to center easily). Skim when necessary throughout cooking, and add more hot water when needed to keep the tongue covered. Lift tongue from pan and plunge into cold water. Remove outer skin and cut off any bones and gristle from root of tongue. Place tongue in a deep, round cake tin or other container about 6-inches in diameter and curl round to the shape of the tin. Cover tongue with a plate and place a weight on top. Chill thoroughly for at least 24 hours and unmould to serve. The weight should press out liquid to form some aspic jelly, but a little strained stock may be added, just barely enough to cover it.
TIME 3 hours to cook, 24 hours to chill.
GARNISH WITH lettuce or watercress.
SERVE WITH pickles or chutney, pickled beet salad and mixed salad.
NOTE 4 lamb tongues can be prepared in the same way and they take half the time given above to cook.

USE YOUR IMAGINATION

Formal table settings with starched table napkins and a vast collection of cutlery and tableware are no longer practical or even desirable for modern living. An occasional formal dinner party can be a wonderful experience for guests and host and hostess, but so can a modern, informal gathering of friends where the conversation is lively and the table setting is simple and attractive.

Modern china and cutlery looks as good on a scrubbed wooden table top as on a starched white damask cloth. A centrepiece for a dinner party can be a basketful of daisies, a collection of candles, or a big soup tureen full of hot soup. The homemaker can be as inventive as she pleases when setting her table. An enormous range of tableware, ovenware and cutlery is available today. When choosing tableware, young home-makers should look for durability as well as attractive appearance, and dishes which come from the oven to the table in style. Good tableware should stack easily if possible, and the colour and design should complement the food you are serving. Table settings for any meal of the day should look uncluttered, colourful, practical as well as pretty. Tablemats are as attractive and functional as tablecloths, whether they are made of raffia, furnishing fabric or material remnants (coated with a water and grease repellent) or laminated materials. Modern stainless steel cutlery can be extremely well designed and requires less upkeep than silver.

BREAKFAST TABLE

Sometimes the homemaker has about five minutes to set a breakfast table, for a family which is on its way to school or work in a hurry. However it is worth the extra five minutes to set a welcoming table with brightly coloured bowls, plates, mugs or large breakfast cups, and a sustaining breakfast is more likely to be eaten and enjoyed. Yellow, orange and warm earth colours are cheerful for the first meal of the day, and a small bunch of homely flowers from the garden—geraniums and nasturtiums—make centrepiece which is sure to be noticed with approval.

LUNCH TABLE

Lunch is sometimes the main meal of the day. If your basic dinner service is simple in colour, design and decoration you can combine it with other dishes to give subtle or bold contrasts. If you are buying a dinner service for the first time, it is a good idea to choose one which is stackable. Meat platters and vegetable dishes should be ovenproof, so that food can be kept hot until ready to be served. When setting the table, try to allow 24 inches of table space for each person. Most placemats are 18 inches wide. Place the cutlery for each person, starting at the outside for the first course and work towards the plate for subsequent courses. The cutlery for dessert can be placed on the inside of the large dinner knife and fork, or it may be placed above the plate position. Glasses are placed to the right of the cutlery, in line with the tip of the large dinner knife. All the cutlery should, for perfection, be placed neatly parallel and the bases should be in line one inch from the edge of the table. A bread plate may be set to the left of each place setting, with a neatly folded serviette on it. A bread roll may be put on top of the serviette. Any serving spoons needed by the hostess may be placed on the table just in front of her place setting. Servers for vegetables, salads, mustard and chutney etc. should be placed on the table beside the appropriate food.

The first course such as fruit juice or soup (if it is cold) may be put on the table before the family is seated. When ready to serve the main course, the meat is placed directly in front of whoever is carving, with a pile of warm dinner plates directly in front to serve onto. Plates are passed to the family or guests, who help themselves to vegetables, gravy etc.

After the main course is finished, the table is cleared of plates and serving dishes and cruet. The dessert is served by the hostess at the table, or both carving of meat and serving of dessert can be done on a sideboard or sidetable if preferred.

DINNER TABLE

The atmosphere you want is helped by the way you set your table. Create a festive atmosphere for a dinner party with candle-light, polished glass, softly arranged flowers and background music. If you have a beautiful wooden dining table, show it to advantage with table mats. If the table is marked, use a cloth. Be inventive—make your own cloth from rich felt, furnishing fabric or hessian, or anything else which pleases your eye. Be clever with contrast — plain linen with patterned tableware, patterned or brightly coloured cloth or mats with plain white china.

If the dinner party is informal, the hostess makes her own rules, and the more inventive she is, the better. A fondue party is fun, with small cubes of steak being cooked at the table by the guests, while the hostess provides assorted sauces and salads. A cheese fondue is ideal for a luncheon party—guests dip crusty pieces of bread in a rich warm cheese mixture. Brightly coloured paper napkins are a good idea for this sort of party, or for a barbecue.

A barbecue on a summer night is a tried and true American tradition, and a very pleasant way for families to share a meal together. A table set outside can be very romantic. Candles protected from stray breezes by old-fashioned glass shields look attractive, and tableware can be as informal as the hostess likes. Fruit and flowers make attractive centerpieces and fresh green salads tossed in wooden bowls are ideal with barbecued steak.

A formal dinner party needs more formal rules. The host sits at the 'top' of the table, the hostess at the other end nearest the kitchen. The female guest of honour sits at the host's right hand, and the male guest of honour at the hostess's right hand. Partners should be separated, a man between each lady.

When serving guests at a formal dinner party, the lady guest of honour is served first, the host and the person on her right are served next. Then guests are served quickly working down the table on each side of the host and hostess. As soon as the hostess is served, then it is in order to start to eat. Most people today insist on their guests eating as soon as they are served, so that the food does not cool.

The host usually serves the wine at any dinner party.

SERVICE OF WINE

The general rule is to serve red wine with red meat such as beef, and white wine with white meat such as veal, lamb and pork, in order to complement the strong or delicate flavors of the meat. Red wine should be served at room temperature, except on a hot summer day when most wine experts agree the wine should be slightly chilled. When serving at room temperature the red wine should be uncorked and allowed to stand in a warm kitchen near the stove for thirty minutes to allow the flavor and bouquet to develop.

White wine should be served chilled. Wine can be served from the bottle or poured in carafes or decanters. This is a matter of personal choice. Spirits, such as whisky or brandy are often kept in small decanters, and wine is often served in larger decanters or small carafes, which hold enough for one person. These personal carafes are now sold in most large department stores, and are an attractive idea for a dinner party. The carafes are filled with wine and placed beside the wine glass at each table setting, and each guest refills his glass when he likes. If you do not fancy a heavy red burgundy or claret, a light, chilled rosé complements the flavour of red meat well. Be adventurous and use wine in cooking—there are many recipes available which enhance the flavour of meat and add richness to desserts. A little red wine stirred into gravy or to stews and casseroles adds richness and flavour. Dessert wines have been neglected but are coming back into favour. A small glass of marsala, madeira or port is delicious served with dessert.

Wine looks and tastes best when served in polished, clear wine glasses on a stem. A red wine glass is rounded, and a white wine glass is a little taller, thinner and almost tulip shaped. Many people like to break with convention and enjoy a white wine with beef and a red wine with veal. It's all a matter of taste, but try to serve a wine which complements the flavour of your meat.

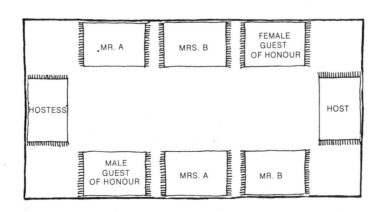

Dry ingredients are given in cups, pounds and ounces and tablespoons. Use the American standard measuring cup. A graduated set of $\frac{1}{4}$ cup, $\frac{1}{3}$ cup, $\frac{1}{2}$ cup and 1 cup is most useful. A good set of scales with avoirdupois weights is also useful. Use the American standard tablespoon.

cup flour	=	1 oz
cup flour	=	2 oz
cup flour	=	3 oz
cup flour	=	4 oz
$\frac{1}{2}$ cups flour	=	6 oz
cups flour	=	8 oz
cups flour	=	12 oz
cups flour	=	1 lb

Liquid measures are given in pints, cups and tablespoons. The American pint is 16 fluid ounces. Use the standard measuring cup which has a capacity of 8 fluid ounces. The measuring cup is marked with a scale of fluid ounces and $\frac{1}{4}$, $\frac{1}{3}$, $\frac{1}{2}$, $\frac{2}{3}$, $\frac{3}{4}$, cup divisions.

1 pint	=	16 fluid oz
$\frac{1}{2}$ pint	=	8 fluid oz
$\frac{1}{4}$ pint	=	4 fluid oz
1 cup	=	8 fluid oz
$\frac{1}{2}$ cup	=	4 fluid oz
$\frac{1}{4}$ cup	=	2 fluid oz
$\frac{1}{8}$ cup	=	1 fluid oz
2 tablespoons	=	1 fluid oz

Common Cookery Measures

3 teaspoons	=	1 tablespoon
4 tablespoons	=	$\frac{1}{4}$ cup
$5\frac{1}{3}$ tablespoons	=	$\frac{1}{3}$ cup
8 tablespoons	=	$\frac{1}{2}$ cup
$10\frac{2}{3}$ tablespoons	=	$\frac{2}{3}$ cup
12 tablespoons	=	$\frac{3}{4}$ cup
16 tablespoons	=	1 cup

Follow the instructions for your own particular range. Different makes vary and even the same makes can give different individual results at the same temperature. The following guide gives the temperature settings for both gas and electric ovens.

	Thermostat Setting °F.	
Description of Oven	Automatic Electric	Gas
Cool	200	200
Very slow	250	250
Slow	300–325	300
Moderately slow	325–350	325
Moderate	350–375	350
Moderately hot	375–400	375
Hot	400–450	400
Very hot	450–500	450

GLOSSARY

BARD
To cover lean meat with strips of fat or fat bacon rashers.

BASTE
To spoon hot dripping over meat occasionally during roasting, to prevent shrinkage and to keep it moist.

BATTER
A mixture of flour and some liquid, egg, milk, or melted butter, in which food is sometimes dipped before deep frying.

BLANCH
To place food in cold water and bring to the boil, then remove food and sometimes transfer to cold water. Certain meats are blanched to remove strong flavor and to improve color.

BLEND
A thickening agent, cornstarch of flour, is mixed to a smooth paste, with cold liquid.

BOUQUET GARNI
A collection of herbs, bay leaf, sprigs of parsley and thyme tied into a bundle with cotton thread or tied in a muslin bag with 6 peppercorns, 2 cloves and 1 blade of mace. Used to add flavor to stews, casseroles, braised meat and soup, and removed before serving.

BRINE
A solution of water in which salt is dissolved. Used for preserving meat.

CLARIFIED BUTTER (GHEE)
Butter is melted over a gentle heat, and the liquid poured off from the sediment. Clarified butter does not burn as readily as unclarified butter as the salt and sediment is removed.

COAT
(1) To cover the surface of food with a coating of seasoned flour, beaten egg and breadcrumbs, or batter, before frying.
(2) To cover food with a coating of sauce.

CROQUETTE
A mixture of chopped food with salt and pepper mixed with a stiff sauce (panada), shaped into a cylinder, coated with flour, egg and breadcrumbs and deep fried.

CROÛTE
A shape of fried bread or toast on which food is served (Tournedos) or which garnishes a savoury dish.

CROUTONS
Small $\frac{1}{4}$-inch cubes of fried or toasted bread, used to accompany soups.

DRIPPING
The fat or drippings yielded when roasting meat.

DUCHESSE
Mashed potatoes mixed with beaten egg and piped into rosettes and baked in a moderate oven until golden, or used to pipe as a decorative border.

GLAZE
To brush pastry with beaten egg or milk before baking, to give a golden color.

LARD
To thread strips of fat into lean meat before cooking.

MARINADE
A mixture of oil and vinegar or wine with seasoned and herbs added. Meat is soaked in the mixture for 1-24 hours to tenderize it and improve the flavor.

PANADA
A very thick white sauce used as a base for croquettes.

PARBOIL
To boil in salted water for approximately 10 minutes.

PASTA
Macaroni, noodles, spaghetti, etc.

PÂTÉ
Finely pounded meat (or fish), often mixed with other ingredients, seasoning and flavoring. Serve cold spread on dry toast.

POPPADUM
Wafer-thin dough fried in oil until crisp and served hot with curry.

REDUCE
To boil or simmer liquid, until, as a result of evaporation of the water content, the volume is reduced.

ROUX
A mixture of melted butter mixed with all-purpose flour and heated gently to burst the starch grains. Made in the preliminary stage of making white sauces and brown sauces.

SAMBALS
The name given to the varied dishes which accompany all curries. They may include sliced banana in lemon juice, chutneys, grated fresh coconut, cucumbers sliced in yoghurt or French dressing, sliced hard-boiled egg, pickles and tomatoes sliced in French dressing.

SEASONING
Salt and pepper.

SEASONED FLOUR
Flour mixed with salt and pepper.

SIMMER
To cook food gently in liquid just below boiling point, with bubbles gently breaking the surface.

SOUR CREAM
Cream that is artificially soured.

STOCK
A liquid containing the nutrients and flavors of meat, bones and vegetables used for making soups, stews, casseroles and gravy.

SUET
A hard fat which surrounds kidneys. It is finely chopped and used in some stuffings and in suet crust pastry.

INDEX